T H E   B O

LIGHT SAUCES
& SALAD DRESSINGS

THE BOOK OF

LIGHT SAUCES
& SALAD DRESSINGS

ANNE SHEASBY

Photographed by
STEVE BAXTER

HPBooks®

ANOTHER BEST-SELLING VOLUME FROM HP BOOKS

HP Books
Published by The Berkley Publishing Group
200 Madison Avenue,
New York, NY 10016.

9 8 7 6 5 4 3 2 1

ISBN: 1-55788-187-1

By arrangement with Salamander Books Ltd.

Home Economist: Carole Handslip
Printed in Belgium by Proost International Book Production

CONTENTS

INTRODUCTION

A good sauce will provide the finishing touch to numerous dishes. A sauce enhances the flavor of food, both sweet and savory, and can transform a dish into something special.

Many sauces are traditionally associated with certain foods, but sauces are also very versatile and can be served with a wide variety of dishes.

More unusual sauces can make a pleasant change and by choosing different ingredients, you can create appetizing sauces to suit all kinds of foods and tastes.

Sauces are simple to make once the basic techniques have been mastered and they don't need to be high in calories or fat to make them appealing and delicious. By replacing some of the more traditional ingredients with lower calorie/lower fat alternatives, you can create light, healthy sauces, full of delicious flavors, colors and textures. You will be reducing your calorie and fat intakes, without even noticing the difference.

In this book, you will discover tasty light sauces, both sweet and savory, plus a delicious selection of light salad dressings. Recipes include traditional sauces as well as more unusual light sauces and each recipe is illustrated in full color with step-by-step instructions, showing you just what to expect.

Try some of these delicious light sauces and add that special finishing touch to your own dishes.

INGREDIENTS FOR LIGHT SAUCES

Today, healthy eating is a very important part of our everyday lives, and following basic, good, healthy eating patterns is essential for our general well-being.

Sauces are often thought of as the delicious, creamy, rich accompaniment to numerous dishes. Traditionally, many sauces have been relatively high in calories and fat, but light sauces, just as delicious and appetizing, can be made by making a few simple changes to the ingredients in the recipe. This results in lower-calorie, reduced-fat, light sauces.

By reducing the amount of fat, sugar, and salt you eat and increasing the amount of fiber in your diet, you will be making small changes in your eating habits, as well as taking positive steps toward a healthier, well-balanced diet.

The recipes use a whole range of different ingredients, all of which are readily available.

LOW-FAT INGREDIENTS

Low-fat spreads, skim or low-fat milk, reduced-fat creams, and reduced-fat cheeses have been used in place of some of the traditional higher-calorie and higher-fat ingredients. Low-fat plain yogurt, for example, is a tasty healthy alternative to milk or cream in some of the light sauces.

In place of butter or margarine, which have very high fat contents, some of the recipes use low-fat margarine. Low-fat spreads contain half the fat of butter or margarine and many are suitable for melting. However, low-fat spreads do vary and you may need to experiment to see which one you like best. Nonfat spreads are not suitable for sauces.

Oil has been used in some of the

recipes, but only the polyunsaturated and monosaturated varieties, such as sunflower oil, sesame oil, and olive oil. Oils are high in calories and fat and should be used sparingly. It is possible to reduce the amount of oil that would traditionally be used in many sauces and dressings without affecting the flavor or texture.

FRUIT & VEGETABLES

Fruit and vegetable purees make excellent low-calorie/low-fat bases for many light sauces, and they add delightful flavors, colors, and textures to many dishes.

Fresh fruits have been used in the recipes as much as possible, as they are full of natural sugar and flavor.

When canned fruit are used in recipes, use canned fruit in fruit juice or light syrup, rather than fruit in a heavy syrup.

Fresh herbs and spices also add delicious flavors and aromas to many of the light sauces, without adding many calories or fat.

SALAD DRESSINGS

The chapter on light salad dressings incorporates a wide choice of delicious dressings for all kinds of salads from simple salad leaves to meat, fish, and pasta salads, all with far fewer calories than traditional salad dressings.

SERVING SUGGESTIONS

Serving suggestions appear at the end of most recipes, but use your imagination – many of the light sauces are very versatile and can be served with a wide variety of dishes.

Each recipe shows the total amount of light sauce the recipe makes, as well as calorie and fat contents per tablespoon or serving.

BASIC WHITE SAUCE

2 tablespoons low-fat margarine
1/4 cup all-purpose flour
1-1/4 cups low-fat milk
Salt and pepper

In a saucepan over low heat, melt low-fat margarine. Stir in flour and cook 1 minute, stirring.

Remove pan from heat and gradually stir or whisk in the milk. Return pan to heat. Bring slowly to a boil, stirring or whisking, and continue to cook until mixture thickens.

Simmer 3 minutes. Remove pan from heat and season with salt and pepper. Serve with meat, poultry, fish, or vegetables.

Makes 1-1/4 cups/20 tablespoons.

Calories per tablespoon: 16
Fat per tablespoon: 0.7 g

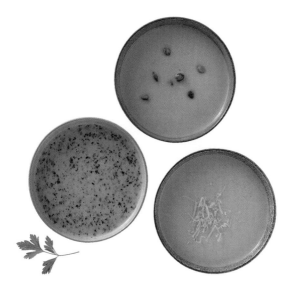

—WHITE SAUCE VARIATIONS—

CHEESE SAUCE
Follow recipe for Basic White Sauce. Before seasoning with salt and pepper, stir in 1/2 cup shredded reduced-fat cheddar cheese and 1 teaspoon prepared mustard. Serve with fish, poultry, ham, vegetables, or egg dishes.

Calories per tablespoon: 23
Fat per tablespoon: 1.2 g

PARSLEY SAUCE
Follow recipe for Basic White Sauce. After seasoning with salt and pepper, stir in 2 tablespoons finely chopped fresh parsley. Serve with fish or ham.

Calories per tablespoon: 16
Fat per tablespoon: 0.7 g

CAPER SAUCE
Follow recipe for Basic White Sauce. Before seasoning with salt and pepper, stir in 2 tablespoons capers and 2 teaspoons vinegar from jar of capers. Reheat gently before serving. Serve with lamb or fish.

Calories per tablespoon: 16
Fat per tablespoon: 0.7 g

ESPAGNOLE SAUCE

1 slice Canadian bacon
2 tablespoons low-fat margarine
1 small onion or shallot
1 small carrot
2 ounces mushrooms
3 tablespoons all-purpose flour
2-1/2 cups beef stock
1 bouquet garni
4 black peppercorns
1 bay leaf
2 tablespoons tomato paste
Salt and pepper

Trim bacon, if needed, then finely chop bacon.

In a saucepan over low heat, melt margarine. Add bacon and cook 2 minutes, stirring. Finely chop onion or shallot, carrot, and mushrooms. Add vegetables to bacon and cook 5 to 10 minutes or until lightly browned, stirring occasionally. Stir in flour and cook until lightly browned, stirring constantly. Remove pan from heat and gradually stir in stock. Add all remaining ingredients, return to heat, and bring slowly to a boil, stirring, until mixture thickens. Cover and simmer 1 hour, stirring occasionally.

Strain sauce, remove bouquet garni, and rub pulp through a strainer. Discard remaining pulp in strainer and return sauce to clean saucepan. Reheat gently and adjust seasoning before serving. Serve with red meats or game.

Makes 1-3/4 cups/28 tablespoons.

Calories per tablespoon: 12
Fat per tablespoon: 0.5 g

BECHAMEL SAUCE

1 small onion or shallot
1 small carrot
1/2 stalk celery
1 bay leaf
6 black peppercorns
Several sprigs parsley
1-1/4 cups low-fat milk
2 tablespoons low-fat margarine
1/4 cup all-purpose flour
Salt and pepper

Slice onion or shallot and carrot. Chop celery roughly. Put vegetables, bay leaf, peppercorns, and parsley into a saucepan with milk and bring slowly to a boil.

Remove pan from heat, cover, and set aside to infuse 30 minutes. Strain into a measuring cup, reserving milk. In a saucepan over low heat, melt margarine. Stir in flour and cook 1 minute, stirring.

Remove pan from heat and gradually stir or whisk in flavored milk. Bring slowly to a boil, stirring or whisking, then continue to cook until mixture thickens. Simmer 3 minutes. Remove pan from heat and season with salt and pepper. Serve with poultry, fish, vegetables, or egg dishes.

Makes 1-1/4 cups/20 tablespoons.

Calories per tablespoon: 18
Fat per tablespoon: 0.8 g

ITALIAN GRAVY

1 small onion
2 tablespoons low-fat margarine
1/4 cup all-purpose flour
1-1/4 cups beef stock
1 tablespoon tomato paste
1 teaspoon sugar
1 teaspoon Italian seasoning
Salt and pepper

Finely chop onion. In a saucepan, over low heat, melt margarine. Add onion and cook 5 minutes or until soft, stirring.

Stir in flour and cook 1 minute, stirring. Remove pan from heat and gradually stir in stock. Add remaining ingredients, return pan to heat, and bring slowly to a boil, stirring. Continue to cook until mixture thickens, then simmer 3 minutes.

Adjust seasoning and serve with broiled or roasted meats, such as beef, lamb, or pork.

Makes 1-3/4 cups/28 tablespoons.

Calories per tablespoon: 9
Fat per tablespoon: 0.4 g

Variation: Use chicken stock instead of beef stock, if serving the gravy with poultry.

ONION SAUCE

1 onion
2 tablespoons low-fat margarine
1/4 cup all-purpose flour
2 cups low-fat milk
Salt and pepper

Chop onion finely. In a saucepan over low heat, melt margarine. Add onion and cook 8 to 10 minutes or until soft, stirring occasionally.

Stir in flour and cook 1 minute, stirring. Remove pan from heat and gradually stir in milk. Return pan to heat and bring slowly to a boil, stirring, then continue to cook until mixture thickens.

Simmer gently 3 minutes. Remove pan from heat and season with salt and pepper. Serve with lamb or egg dishes.

Makes 2-1/4 cups/36 tablespoons.

Calories per tablespoon: 12
Fat per tablespoon: 0.5 g

PIQUANT SAUCE

1 small onion
1 small carrot
2 ounces mushrooms
2 tablespoons low-fat margarine
1/4 cup all-purpose flour
2-1/2 cups vegetable stock
1 bay leaf
Salt and pepper
1 tablespoon capers, drained
1 small dill pickle
1 tablespoon chopped fresh parsley

Finely chop onion, carrot, and mushrooms. In a saucepan over low heat, melt margarine.

Add onion, carrot, and mushrooms and cook 8 to 10 minutes or until soft, stirring occasionally. Stir in flour and cook 1 minute, stirring. Remove pan from heat and gradually stir in stock. Return pan to heat. Bring slowly to a boil, stirring, then continue to cook until mixture thickens. Add bay leaf, salt, and pepper, then cover and simmer 30 minutes, stirring occasionally. Finely chop capers and dill pickle. Remove bay leaf from sauce and discard.

Stir chopped capers, dill pickles, and parsley into sauce. Reheat gently, adjust seasoning and serve with fish or red meats.

Makes 3-1/4 cups/52 tablespoons.

Calories per tablespoon: 5
Fat per tablespoon: 0.2 g

Variation: Use your own mixture of vegetables in this recipe such as tomatoes, green onions, and celery.

———— MUSTARD SAUCE ————

2 tablespoons low-fat margarine
1/4 cup all-purpose flour
1-1/4 cups low-fat milk
2 tablespoons whole-grain mustard
Salt and pepper

In a saucepan over low heat, melt margarine. Stir in flour and cook 1 minute, stirring.

Remove pan from heat and gradually stir or whisk in milk. Return pan to heat. Bring slowly to a boil, stirring or whisking, then continue to cook until mixture thickens. Simmer 3 minutes.

Stir in mustard and season with salt and pepper. Reheat gently before serving. Serve with oily fish, ham, bacon, vegetables, or cheese dishes.

Makes 1-1/2 cups/24 tablespoons.

Calories per tablespoon: 15
Fat per tablespoon: 0.8 g

TARRAGON SAUCE

2 tablespoons low-fat margarine
1/4 cup all-purpose flour
1-1/4 cups chicken stock
2/3 cup low-fat milk
2 tablespoons tarragon vinegar
Few sprigs tarragon
2 teaspoons Dijon mustard
1/2 cup shredded reduced-fat cheddar cheese
Salt and pepper

In a saucepan over low heat, melt margarine. Stir in flour and cook 1 minute, stirring. Remove pan from heat and gradually stir or whisk in stock, milk, and vinegar.

Return pan to heat. Bring slowly to a boil, stirring or whisking, then continue to cook until mixture thickens. Simmer 3 minutes. Finely chop tarragon.

Stir tarragon into sauce along with mustard, cheese, salt, and pepper and reheat gently, but do not let sauce boil. Serve with chicken or turkey.

Makes 2-1/4 cups/36 tablespoons.

Calories per tablespoon: 11
Fat per tablespoon: 0.6 g

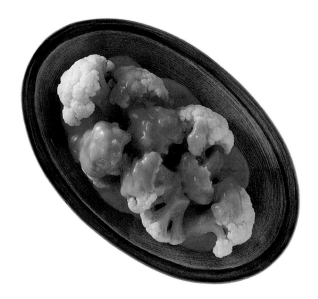

PAPRIKA SAUCE

1 small onion
2 tablespoons low-fat margarine
1/4 cup all-purpose flour
1 teaspoon paprika
3/4 cup low-fat milk
1/3 cup dry sherry
Salt and pepper

Finely chop onion. In a saucepan over low heat, melt margarine. Add onion and cook 5 minutes, stirring.

Whisk in flour and paprika and cook 1 minute, stirring. Remove pan from heat and gradually whisk in milk and sherry.

Return pan to heat. Bring slowly to a boil, whisking, then continue to boil gently 3 minutes. Remove pan from heat and season with salt and pepper. Serve with vegetables such as cauliflower or squash.

Makes 1-1/3 cups/21 tablespoons.

Calories per tablespoon: 19
Fat per tablespoon: 0.7 g

— LEMON & CHERVIL SAUCE —

2 tablespoons low-fat margarine
2 tablespoons all-purpose flour
2/3 cup chicken stock
2/3 cup low-fat milk
Few sprigs chervil
Finely grated zest and juice of 1 lemon
Salt and pepper

In a saucepan over low heat, melt margarine. Stir in flour and cook 1 minute, stirring. Remove pan from heat and gradually stir or whisk in stock and milk.

Return pan to heat. Bring slowly to a boil, stirring or whisking, then continue to cook until mixture thickens. Simmer 3 minutes. Chop chervil finely.

Stir chervil into sauce with lemon zest and juice, and season with salt and pepper. Reheat sauce gently before serving. Serve with fish, such as cod, haddock, flounder, or salmon.

Makes 1-1/4 cups/20 tablespoons.

Calories per tablespoon: 17
Fat per tablespoon: 0.7 g

BORDELAISE SAUCE

1 slice lean bacon
2 tablespoons low-fat margarine
2 shallots
1 carrot
2 ounces mushrooms
3 tablespoons all-purpose flour
1-1/4 cups beef stock
1-1/4 cups red wine
1 bouquet garni
Salt and pepper

Finely chop bacon. In a saucepan over low heat, melt margarine. Add bacon and cook 2 minutes, stirring.

Finely chop shallots, carrot, and mushrooms. Add to bacon and cook 5 to 10 minutes or until lightly browned, stirring occasionally. Add flour and cook until lightly browned, stirring constantly. Remove pan from heat and gradually stir in stock and wine.

Return pan to heat. Bring slowly to a boil, stirring, then continue to cook until mixture thickens. Add bouquet garni and season with salt and pepper. Cover and simmer 1 hour, stirring occasionally. Strain sauce, adjust seasoning, and serve with red meats or game.

Makes 1-2/3 cups/26 tablespoons.

Calories per tablespoon: 21
Fat per tablespoon: 0.5 g

MUSHROOM SAUCE

1 small onion
1 small carrot
1/2 stalk celery
1 bay leaf
6 black peppercorns
2 cups low-fat milk
6 ounces button mushrooms
1/4 cup low-fat margarine
1/2 cup all-purpose flour
Salt and pepper

Slice onion and carrot. Chop celery roughly. Put vegetables, bay leaf, and peppercorns into a saucepan. Add milk and slowly bring to a boil.

Remove pan from heat, cover, and set aside to infuse 30 minutes. Strain into a measuring cup, reserving milk. Slice mushrooms thinly. In a saucepan over low heat, melt margarine. Add mushrooms and cook 5 minutes or until soft, stirring occasionally. Stir in flour and cook 1 minute, stirring. Remove pan from heat and gradually stir in flavored milk.

Return pan to heat. Bring slowly to a boil, stirring, then continue to cook until mixture thickens. Simmer 3 minutes. Remove pan from heat and season with salt and pepper. Serve with fish or vegetables, such as broccoli or potatoes.

Makes 2-1/4 cups/36 tablespoons.

Calories per tablespoon: 18
Fat per tablespoon: 0.9 g

RED WINE SAUCE

1 small onion
1 garlic clove
2 tablespoons low-fat margarine
1/4 cup all-purpose flour
1 cup beef stock
3/4 cup red wine
2 teaspoons chopped fresh thyme
1 tablespoon lemon juice
Salt and pepper

Grate onion finely and crush garlic. In a saucepan over low heat, melt margarine. Add onion and garlic and cook 5 minutes, stirring occasionally.

Stir in flour and cook 1 minute, stirring. Remove pan from heat and gradually stir in stock and wine. Return pan to heat. Bring slowly to a boil, stirring, then continue to cook until mixture thickens. Simmer 3 minutes.

Stir chopped thyme into sauce along with lemon juice and season with salt and pepper. Reheat sauce gently before serving. Serve with beef.

Makes 2 cups/32 tablespoons.

Calories per tablespoon: 10
Fat per tablespoon: 0.3 g

Variation: Use medium-dry white wine in place of red wine to make a white wine sauce and serve it with poultry or fish.

CELERY SAUCE

1 small onion
8 ounces celery
2 tablespoons low-fat margarine
1/4 cup all-purpose flour
2/3 cup low-fat milk
2/3 cup vegetable stock
Salt and pepper

Finely chop onion and celery. In a saucepan over low heat, melt margarine.

Add onion and celery to pan and cook 8 to 10 minutes or until soft, stirring occasionally. Stir in flour and cook 1 minute, stirring. Remove pan from heat and gradually stir in milk and stock. Return pan to heat. Bring slowly to a boil, stirring, then continue to cook until mixture thickens.

Simmer 3 minutes. Remove pan from heat and season with salt and pepper. Serve with roast chicken or turkey.

Makes 2-1/4 cups/36 tablespoons.

Calories per tablespoon: 8
Fat per tablespoon: 0.4 g

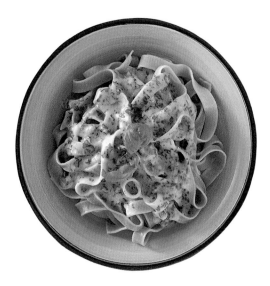

FRESH BASIL SAUCE

1 small onion or shallot
1 garlic clove
1 tablespoon low-fat margarine
2 tablespoons all-purpose flour
1-1/4 cups low-fat milk
1 ounce fresh Parmesan cheese
2 tablespoons chopped fresh basil
Salt and pepper

Finely chop onion or shallot and crush garlic. In a saucepan over low heat, melt margarine. Add onion or shallot and garlic and cook 5 minutes, stirring.

Stir in flour and cook 1 minute, stirring. Remove pan from heat and gradually whisk in milk. Return pan to heat. Bring slowly to a boil, whisking, then continue to cook until mixture thickens. Simmer 3 minutes. Grate Parmesan cheese.

Whisk basil and Parmesan cheese into sauce and season with salt and pepper. Reheat gently before serving. Serve with chicken, fish, or pasta.

Makes 1-1/2 cups/24 tablespoons.

Calories per tablespoon: 16
Fat per tablespoon: 0.8 g

QUICK TOMATO SAUCE

1 garlic clove
1 tablespoon chopped mixed fresh herbs such as
    parsley, thyme, rosemary, and chives
1 (15-1/2-oz.) can crushed tomatoes
2/3 cup dry white wine
1 tablespoon tomato paste
Salt and pepper
1 tablespoon cornstarch

Crush garlic. Combine garlic, herbs, tomatoes, wine, tomato paste, salt, and pepper in a saucepan.

Bring slowly to a boil, then reduce heat, cover, and simmer 20 minutes, stirring occasionally. In a small bowl, blend cornstarch with 1 tablespoon water.

Stir cornstarch mixture into tomato sauce, mixing together well, then bring sauce back to a boil, stirring. Simmer 3 minutes. Adjust seasoning before serving. Serve with fish, meat, or poultry.

Makes 2-1/4 cups/36 tablespoons.

Calories per tablespoon: 6
Fat per tablespoon: 0.02 g

WATERCRESS SAUCE

1 small onion
1 garlic clove
2 bunches watercress
2 tablespoons low-fat margarine
1/4 cup all-purpose flour
1-1/4 cups low-fat milk
2/3 cup chicken stock
Salt and pepper

Finely chop onion. Crush garlic and finely chop watercress. In a saucepan over low heat, melt margarine. Add onion, garlic, and watercress and cook 5 minutes or until soft, stirring occasionally.

Stir in flour and cook 1 minute, stirring. Remove pan from heat and gradually stir or whisk in milk and stock, and season with salt and pepper. Bring slowly to a boil, stirring or whisking, then continue to cook until mixture thickens. Cover and simmer 5 minutes, stirring occasionally. Remove pan from heat and set aside to cool.

When cool, in a blender or food processor, puree sauce until smooth. Return sauce to clean saucepan, reheat gently, and adjust seasoning before serving. Serve with lamb, fish, or savory pies or quiches.

Makes 2-1/4 cups/36 tablespoons.

Calories per tablespoon: 8
Fat per tablespoon: 0.4 g

— MUSHROOM & SAGE SAUCE —

2 shallots
12 ounces brown mushrooms
2 teaspoons olive oil
1-1/4 cups vegetable stock
1-1/4 cups low-fat milk
2 tablespoons chopped fresh sage
1 bay leaf
Salt and pepper
1 tablespoon cornstarch

Finely chop shallots and mushrooms. In a saucepan, heat oil 1 minute. Add shallots and mushrooms and cook 8 to 10 minutes or until soft, stirring.

Stir in stock and milk. Add chopped sage to saucepan with bay leaf and season with salt and pepper, mixing together well. Bring slowly to a boil, then cover and simmer 30 minutes, stirring occasionally. Remove and discard bay leaf.

In a small bowl, blend cornstarch with 2 tablespoons cold water. Stir cornstarch mixture into sauce and bring slowly back to a boil, stirring constantly. Simmer 3 minutes and adjust seasoning before serving. Serve with chicken, fish, or veal.

Makes 3-3/4 cups/60 tablespoons.

Calories per tablespoon: 6
Fat per tablespoon: 0.3 g

——RED BELL PEPPER SAUCE——

2 red bell peppers (see Note)
6 green onions
2 garlic cloves
1 sprig rosemary
1-1/4 cups vegetable stock
Salt and pepper

Seed bell peppers and chop finely. Trim and slice green onions thinly. Crush garlic and finely chop rosemary. Put peppers, green onions, garlic, rosemary, stock, salt, and pepper into a saucepan.

Bring mixture slowly to a boil, reduce heat, cover, and simmer 20 minutes or until vegetables are soft, stirring occasionally. Remove pan from heat and set aside to cool. When slightly cool, in a blender or food processor, puree sauce until smooth. Return sauce to clean saucepan.

Reheat gently and adjust seasoning before serving. Serve hot or cold with vegetable dishes such as a vegetable terrine.

Makes 2 cups/32 tablespoons.

Calories per tablespoon: 4
Fat per tablespoon: 0.06 g

Note: The peppers may be peeled if wished. Place under a hot broiler and broil 8 to 10 minutes, turning frequently. Rub off skins under cold water.

— CARROT & CILANTRO SAUCE —

1 onion
1 pound carrots
2 teaspoons sunflower oil
2 tablespoons chopped fresh cilantro
1-1/4 cups vegetable stock
Salt and pepper

Finely chop onion and coarsely grate carrots. In a saucepan, heat oil 1 minute. Add onion and carrots and cook 8 minutes, stirring.

Add chopped cilantro to carrots along with stock, salt, and pepper. Bring slowly to a boil, then cover and simmer 15 to 20 minutes, stirring occasionally. Remove pan from heat and set aside to cool.

When slightly cool, in a blender or food processor, puree sauce until smooth. Return sauce to clean saucepan. Reheat gently and adjust seasoning before serving. Serve with poultry or game.

Makes 3-1/4 cups/52 tablespoons.

Calories per tablespoon: 6
Fat per tablespoon: 0.2 g

Variation: Use different herbs in place of cilantro, such as parsley, thyme, or chives.

HORSERADISH SAUCE

4 tablespoons grated fresh horseradish
1 teaspoon sugar
2 teaspoons Dijon mustard
Salt and pepper
2 tablespoons malt vinegar
3 tablespoons low-fat plain yogurt

Place the grated horseradish into a bowl. Add sugar, mustard, salt, and pepper and mix together well.

Stir in vinegar, then gently stir in yogurt, mixing together well. Leave horseradish sauce in a cool place 30 minutes before serving to let flavors develop.

Serve with beef or oily fish.

Makes 2/3 cup/10 tablespoons.

Calories per tablespoon: 10
Fat per tablespoon: 0.1 g

CHILE SAUCE

4 green onions
1 red chile
1 garlic clove
1 tablespoon peanut oil
1 (14-1/2-oz.) can crushed tomatoes
1 tablespoon lemon juice
1 tablespoon light brown sugar
Salt and pepper
2 teaspoons cornstarch

Trim and finely chop green onions. Seed and finely chop chile and crush garlic.

In a saucepan, heat oil 1 minute. Add onions, chile, and garlic and cook 5 minutes, stirring. Add tomatoes, lemon juice, sugar, salt, and pepper. Bring slowly to a boil, then cover and simmer 10 minutes, stirring occasionally.

In a small bowl, blend cornstarch with 1 tablespoon water. Stir cornstarch mixture into chile sauce and bring sauce to a boil, stirring constantly. Simmer 3 minutes and adjust seasoning before serving. Serve with fish, seafood, or stuffed vegetables.

Makes 1-3/4 cups/28 tablespoons.

Calories per tablespoon: 11
Fat per tablespoon: 0.5 g

──SPINACH & GARLIC SAUCE──

10 ounces fresh spinach
2/3 cup vegetable stock
4 garlic cloves
1 tablespoon chopped mixed fresh herbs, such as
    parsley, thyme, rosemary, and chives
1 teaspoon ground cumin
Salt and pepper

Using a sharp knife, chop spinach roughly, then place in a saucepan with stock. Cover saucepan, bring mixture to a boil, and boil 5 minutes or until spinach is soft. Crush garlic cloves.

Stir garlic, herbs, cumin, salt, and pepper into spinach mixture, mixing together well. Bring slowly to a boil, then cover and simmer 10 minutes, stirring occasionally. Remove pan from heat and set aside to cool.

When slightly cool, in a blender or food processor, puree sauce until smooth. Return sauce to saucepan. Reheat gently and adjust seasoning before serving. Serve with beef, fish, or egg dishes.

Makes 2 cups/32 tablespoons.

Calories per tablespoon: 3
Fat per tablespoon: 0.1 g

──────── CURRY SAUCE ────────

1 onion
1 garlic clove
2 teaspoons sunflower oil
8 ounces potatoes
1 (8-oz.) can crushed tomatoes
1-1/4 cups vegetable stock
1 tablespoon curry powder
1 teaspoon ground bay leaves
Salt and pepper
1/3 cup golden raisins

Finely chop onion and crush garlic. In a saucepan, heat oil 1 minute. Add onion and garlic and cook 5 minutes, stirring.

Peel and coarsely grate potatoes. Add potatoes, tomatoes, stock, curry powder, ground bay leaves, salt, and pepper to saucepan and mix together well. Bring slowly to a boil, then cover and simmer 30 minutes, stirring occasionally. Remove pan from heat and set aside to cool. When slightly cool, in a blender or food processor, puree sauce until smooth.

Return sauce to clean saucepan and add golden raisins. Reheat gently and adjust seasoning before serving. Serve with vegetables or egg dishes.

Makes 3-1/4 cups/52 tablespoons.

Calories per tablespoon: 11
Fat per tablespoon: 0.2 g

Variation: The golden raisins can be added with potatoes and tomatoes and pureed, if preferred.

—— PARSLEY & CHIVE SAUCE ——

2 tablespoons low-fat margarine
1/4 cup all-purpose flour
1-1/4 cups low-fat milk
2 tablespoons chopped fresh parsley
2 tablespoons snipped fresh chives
Salt and pepper

In a saucepan over low heat, melt margarine.
Stir in flour and cook 1 minute, stirring.

Remove pan from heat and gradually whisk in
milk. Return pan to heat. Bring slowly to a
boil, whisking, then continue to cook until
mixture thickens.

Simmer 3 minutes. Remove pan from heat
and stir in herbs and season with salt and
pepper. Serve with ham or fish.

Makes 1-1/2 cups/24 tablespoons.

Calories per tablespoon: 14
Fat per tablespoon: 0.7 g

—SAGE & RED ONION SAUCE—

2 red onions
2 tablespoons low-fat margarine
1/4 cup all-purpose flour
2/3 cup low-fat milk
Juice of 1 lime
2 tablespoons chopped fresh sage
Salt and pepper

Using a sharp knife, finely chop onions. Put onions in a saucepan with 1-1/4 cups water. Bring to a boil, then reduce heat, cover, and simmer 10 minutes or until onions are soft. Strain onions, reserving 2/3 cup of the cooking liquid.

In a saucepan over low heat, melt margarine. Add onions and cook 5 minutes, stirring. Stir in flour and cook 1 minute, stirring. Remove pan from heat and gradually stir in reserved stock, the milk, and lime juice.

Return pan to heat. Bring slowly to a boil, stirring, then continue to cook until mixture thickens. Simmer 3 minutes. Remove pan from heat. Stir chopped sage into sauce. Season with salt and pepper, mixing together well. Serve with poultry or game.

Makes 2 cups/32 tablespoons.

Calories per tablespoon: 11
Fat per tablespoon: 0.4 g

— BROCCOLI & CHEESE SAUCE —

8 ounces broccoli
1 tablespoon cornstarch
1 cup dry white wine
1 garlic clove
2/3 cup low-fat cream cheese
Salt and pepper

Trim broccoli, then cook in a saucepan of boiling water 10 minutes or until tender. Drain, reserving 2 tablespoons of the cooking liquid. Cool broccoli, then, in a blender or food processor, puree with reserved liquid until smooth. Set pureed broccoli aside.

In a saucepan, blend cornstarch and wine. Crush garlic and add to wine mixture. Bring slowly to a boil, stirring constantly, until mixture thickens. Simmer 3 minutes.

Remove pan from heat and stir in cream cheese, pureed broccoli, salt, and pepper, Return pan to heat and mix together well. Reheat gently. Adjust seasoning before serving. Serve hot or cold with poultry, beef, or fish.

Makes 2-1/4 cups/36 tablespoons.

Calories per tablespoon: 13
Fat per tablespoon: 0.6 g

——— SPICY ZUCCHINI SAUCE ———

2 zucchini
1 green bell pepper
1 small onion
1 garlic clove
2 tablespoons low-fat margarine
1 teaspoon ground coriander
1/2 teaspoon ground cumin
1/2 teaspoon chili powder
1/4 teaspoon red (cayenne) pepper
1/4 teaspoon turmeric
2/3 cup vegetable stock
Salt and pepper

Trim the zucchini, then coarsely grate them.

Seed and finely chop bell pepper. Finely chop onion and crush garlic. In a saucepan over low heat, melt margarine. Add zucchini, bell pepper, onion, and garlic and cook 5 minutes, stirring.

Stir in spices, stock, salt, and pepper and mix well. Bring slowly to a boil, then cover and simmer 25 minutes, stirring occasionally. Remove pan from heat and set aside to cool. When slightly cool, in a blender or food processor, puree mixture until smooth. Return sauce to clean saucepan. Reheat gently and adjust seasoning before serving. Serve with shellfish, fish, or meat.

Makes 2 cups/32 tablespoons.

Calories per tablespoon: 8
Fat per tablespoon: 0.4 g

BEET & ORANGE SAUCE

1 small onion or shallot
2 stalks celery
2 teaspoons sunflower oil
1 pound uncooked beets
1-1/4 cups vegetable stock
1 bay leaf
Finely grated zest and juice of 1 orange
1 tablespoon chopped fresh parsley
Salt and pepper
2/3 cup sour cream

Using a sharp knife, finely chop onion or shallot and celery. In a saucepan, heat oil 1 minute. Add onion or shallot and celery and cook 3 minutes, stirring.

Peel and dice beets. Add to saucepan and cook 3 minutes, stirring. Stir in stock and bay leaf and mix together well. Bring slowly to a boil, then reduce heat, cover and simmer 1 to 1-1/2 hours or until beets are soft. Remove and discard bay leaf. Stir orange zest, orange juice, and parsley into sauce and mix together well. Remove pan from heat and set aside to cool.

When slightly cool, in a blender or food processor, puree mixture until smooth. Return sauce to clean saucepan. Reheat gently and season with salt and pepper. Remove pan from heat and stir in sour cream just before serving. Serve hot or cold with turkey, veal, or oily fish.

Makes 3-1/4 cups/52 tablespoons.

Calories per tablespoon: 11
Fat per tablespoon: 0.8 g

SALSA

2 garlic cloves
1 fresh hot red chile
2 tablespoons chopped mixed fresh herbs, such as
     parsley, thyme, rosemary, and chives
1 (14-1/2-oz.) can crushed tomatoes
Juice of 1 lime
Salt and pepper

Crush garlic, and seed and finely chop chile.

Combine garlic, chile, chopped herbs, tomatoes, lime juice, salt, and pepper in a saucepan.

Bring slowly to a boil, then reduce heat and simmer, uncovered, 10 minutes, stirring occasionally. The salsa may be served hot or cold. Serve with Mexican foods, such as filled tortillas.

Makes 3/4 cup/12 tablespoons.

Calories per tablespoon: 8
Fat per tablespoon: 0.07 g

──APPLESAUCE WITH MINT──

1 small onion
1 pound cooking apples
Small bunch fresh mint
2 tablespoons sugar

Using a sharp knife, finely chop onion. Peel, core, and slice apples. Put onion, apples, and 2 tablespoons water into a saucepan.

Cover saucepan and simmer until apples and onion are soft, stirring occasionally. Remove pan from heat and mash apples and onion lightly together.

Using a sharp knife, finely chop mint. Add mint to saucepan with sugar, mixing together well. Reheat sauce gently, stirring until sugar dissolves. Serve hot or cold with lamb or pork.

Makes 1-2/3 cups/26 tablespoons.

Calories per tablespoon: 11
Fat per tablespoon: 0.03 g

——— FRESH TOMATO SAUCE ———

6 green onions
1 carrot
1 stalk celery
1 garlic clove
1 teaspoon olive oil
1-1/2 pounds tomatoes, peeled and chopped
1 tablespoon chopped fresh mixed herbs, such as
    parsley, thyme, rosemary, and chives
1 teaspoon ground bay leaves
1 teaspoon sugar
2 tablespoons tomato paste (optional)
Salt and pepper

Using a sharp knife, finely chop green onions, carrot, and celery. Crush garlic.

In a saucepan, heat oil 1 minute. Add onions, carrot, celery, and garlic and cook 5 minutes, stirring. Add tomatoes to pan with remaining ingredients. Bring slowly to a boil, then cover and simmer 15 minutes, stirring occasionally. Remove pan from heat and set aside to cool. When slightly cool, in a blender or food processor, puree mixture until smooth. Strain pureed sauce through a nylon strainer, discarding pulp. Return sauce to saucepan. Reheat gently and adjust seasoning before serving.

Serve with Greek dishes, such as stuffed grape leaves or meatballs.

Makes 2 cups/32 tablespoons.

Calories per tablespoon: 8
Fat per tablespoon: 0.2 g

Note: A simple way to peel tomatoes is to place them in boiling water about 30 seconds, then plunge them into cold water. The skins should then slip off easily.

——DILL & CUCUMBER SAUCE——

1/2 hot-house or European cucumber
1 tablespoon chopped fresh dill
1-1/4 cups low-fat plain yogurt
1 teaspoon Dijon mustard
Salt and pepper

Using a sharp knife, finely chop cucumber. Into a bowl, place cucumber and chopped dill, mixing together well.

Stir in plain yogurt and mustard and mix together well. Season with salt and pepper. Let sauce stand in a cool place 30 minutes before serving to let flavors develop.

Serve with white fish, oily fish, or shellfish.

Makes 2 cups/32 tablespoons.

Calories per tablespoon: 6
Fat per tablespoon: 0.1 g

SPICY LENTIL SAUCE

1 onion
1 carrot
2 stalks celery
2 teaspoons olive oil
1-1/3 cups green lentils
1 tablespoon chopped fresh parsley
1 teaspoon ground cumin
1 teaspoon ground coriander
1 teaspoon ground allspice
1 teaspoon red (cayenne) pepper
Salt and pepper
2-1/2 cups vegetable stock
3 tablespoons medium-dry sherry

Finely chop onion, carrot, and celery.

In a saucepan, heat oil 1 minute. Add onion, carrot, celery, and lentils and cook 10 minutes, stirring. Stir in parsley, spices, salt, pepper, stock, and sherry and mix together well. Bring slowly to a boil, then cover and simmer 1 hour or until lentils are soft, stirring occasionally.

Remove pan from heat and set aside to cool. When slightly cool, in a blender or food processor, puree mixture until smooth. Return sauce to clean saucepan. Reheat gently and adjust seasoning before serving. Serve with Middle Eastern dishes, such as meatballs or kebabs.

Makes 3-1/2 cups/56 tablespoons.

Calories per tablespoon: 17
Fat per tablespoon: 0.3 g

—GREEN PEPPERCORN SAUCE—

1 tablespoon low-fat margarine
2 tablespoons all-purpose flour
2/3 cup vegetable stock
2/3 cup low-fat milk
1 tablespoon dried green peppercorns
1/4 cup finely shredded smoked cheese
Salt and pepper

In a saucepan over low heat, melt margarine.
Stir in flour and cook 1 minute, whisking.

Remove pan from heat and gradually whisk in
stock and milk. Return pan to heat. Bring
slowly to a boil, whisking, then continue to
cook until mixture thickens. Simmer 3
minutes. Remove pan from heat. Chop or
crush peppercorns.

Stir peppercorns and cheese into sauce.
Season with salt and pepper and reheat
gently, but do not let sauce boil. Serve with
pork, lamb, or poultry.

Makes 1-1/2 cups/24 tablespoons

Calories per tablespoon: 12
Fat per tablespoon: 0.8 g

—— YELLOW PEPPER SAUCE ——

2 yellow bell peppers, chopped
1/2 mild green chile, seeded and finely chopped
1 tablespoon chopped mixed fresh herbs, such as
    parsley, thyme, rosemary, and chives
1-1/4 cups vegetable stock
2 tablespoons medium-dry white wine
Salt and pepper
1 tablespoon cornstarch

Put peppers, chile, herbs, stock, wine, salt, and pepper into a saucepan and mix together well.

Bring slowly to a boil, then cover and simmer 10 minutes, stirring occasionally. Remove pan from heat and set aside to cool. When slightly cool, in a blender or food processor, puree mixture until smooth. Return sauce to clean saucepan. In a small bowl, blend cornstarch with 2 tablespoons water.

Stir cornstarch mixture into pepper sauce and heat gently until sauce thickens, stirring constantly. Simmer 3 minutes. Remove pan from heat and adjust seasoning before serving. Serve with lamb or vegetables, such as asparagus, broccoli, or corn.

Makes 2 cups/32 tablespoons.

Calories per tablespoon: 5
Fat per tablespoon: 0.03 g

──── TOMATO & BASIL SAUCE ────

6 green onions
1 garlic clove
2 teaspoons olive oil
1 pound tomatoes, peeled and chopped
2 tablespoons chopped fresh basil
1 tablespoon tomato paste
1/2 teaspoon sugar
1/4 cup medium-dry sherry
Salt and pepper

Finely chop green onions and crush garlic. In a saucepan, heat oil 1 minute. Add onions and garlic and cook 5 minutes, stirring.

Add tomatoes to saucepan, mixing together well. Stir basil, tomato paste, sugar, sherry, salt, and pepper into tomato mixture and mix together well.

Bring slowly to a boil, then cover and simmer 20 minutes, stirring occasionally. Adjust the seasoning before serving. Serve with fresh filled pasta, such as tortellini or ravioli.

Makes 2-1/2 cups/40 tablespoons.

Calories per tablespoon: 7
Fat per tablespoon: 0.3 g

Variation: Use canned tomatoes in place of fresh tomatoes.

PEA & CORN SAUCE

1 onion
2 tablespoons low-fat margarine
2-1/2 cups frozen green peas
2/3 cup vegetable stock
1/2 teaspoon ground cumin
1 (8-oz.) can whole-kernel corn
1 tablespoon sesame seeds
Salt and pepper

Using a sharp knife, finely chop onion. In a saucepan over low heat, melt margarine. Add onion and cook 5 minutes, stirring. Stir in peas, stock, and cumin, mixing together well. Bring slowly to a boil, then cover and simmer 15 minutes.

Remove pan from heat and set aside to cool. When slightly cool, in a blender or food processor, puree mixture until smooth. Return sauce to clean saucepan. Drain corn and stir into sauce.

Stir in sesame seeds and season with salt and pepper. Reheat sauce gently and adjust seasoning before serving. Serve with fish or poultry.

Makes 2-3/4 cups/44 tablespoons.

Calories per tablespoon: 17
Fat per tablespoon: 0.6 g

PIZZA SAUCE

1 onion
1 garlic clove
2 teaspoons olive oil
1 red bell pepper, diced
6 ounces mushrooms, sliced
1 pound tomatoes, peeled and chopped
1 tablespoon red-wine vinegar
1 teaspoon sugar
1-1/2 teaspoons dried basil
1-1/2 teaspoons dried oregano
Salt and pepper

Slice onion and crush garlic. In a saucepan, heat oil 1 minute. Add onion and garlic and cook 3 minutes, stirring.

Add bell pepper, mushrooms, tomatoes, vinegar, sugar, herbs, salt, and pepper to saucepan and mix together well. Bring slowly to a boil, then reduce heat, cover, and simmer 20 minutes, stirring occasionally.

Remove cover and boil sauce rapidly 10 minutes to thicken, stirring occasionally. Adjust seasoning before serving. Serve as a topping on a pizza crust.

Makes 3-1/2 cups/56 tablespoons.

Calories per tablespoon: 7
Fat per tablespoon: 0.3 g

Variation: Add your own choice of chopped vegetables or chopped cooked meat to basic pizza sauce recipe.

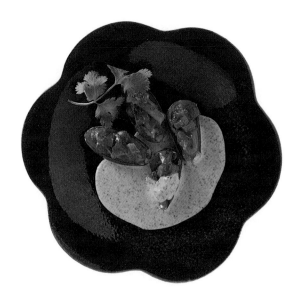

—CREAMY RED BEAN SAUCE—

1 small red onion
Few sprigs parsley
Few sprigs thyme
2 tablespoons low-fat margarine
2 (15-oz.) cans red kidney beans
2/3 cup vegetable stock
Juice of 1 lemon
Salt and pepper
1/4 cup sour cream

Using a sharp knife, finely chop onion and herbs. In a saucepan over low heat, melt margarine. Add onion and cook 3 minutes, stirring.

Drain and rinse kidney beans. Stir kidney beans, stock, lemon juice, herbs, salt, and pepper into saucepan, mixing together well. Bring slowly to a boil, then cover and simmer 10 minutes, stirring occasionally. Remove pan from heat and set aside to cool.

When slightly cool, in a blender or food processor, puree mixture. Return sauce to clean saucepan and reheat gently. Adjust seasoning and stir in sour cream just before serving. Serve with meat or vegetables.

Makes 3-1/4 cups/52 tablespoons.

Calories per tablespoon: 21
Fat per tablespoon: 0.5g

Variation: Use other canned beans or legumes in place of kidney beans.

BLACK BEAN SAUCE

1 (1-inch) piece ginger root
2 teaspoons sesame oil
1 mild green chile, seeded and finely chopped
4 green onions, finely chopped
1 garlic clove, crushed
2 ounces fermented black beans
1-1/4 cups vegetable stock
Salt and pepper
1 tablespoon cornstarch

Peel and finely chop ginger root. In a sauce-pan, heat oil 1 minute.

Add chile, green onions, garlic, and ginger root, then cook 5 minutes, stirring. Stir in beans, stock, salt, and pepper and mix together well. Bring slowly to a boil, reduce heat, cover, and simmer 10 minutes, stirring occasionally. In a small bowl, blend corn-starch with 1 tablespoon water.

Stir cornstarch mixture into sauce and bring slowly to a boil, stirring constantly. Simmer 3 minutes and adjust seasoning before serving. Serve with Chinese-style dishes.

Makes 1-3/4 cups/28 tablespoons.

Calories per tablespoon: 16
Fat per tablespoon: 0.9 g

Note: Fermented black beans are available in Chinese supermarkets, or the Oriental food section of some large supermarkets.

FENNEL & OLIVE SAUCE

2 fennel bulbs
2 tablespoons low-fat margarine
1/4 cup all-purpose flour
1-1/4 cups low-fat milk
20 pitted ripe olives, sliced
1 teaspoon dried dill
Salt and pepper

Trim and quarter fennel, then cook in 1-1/4 cups boiling water 15 to 20 minutes or until soft. Drain, reserving 2/3 cup of the cooking liquid. Set cooked fennel aside to cool, then, in a blender or food processor, puree with 3 tablespoons of the cooking liquid.

In a saucepan over low heat, melt margarine. Stir in flour and cook 1 minute, stirring. Remove pan from heat and gradually stir or whisk in remaining reserved cooking liquid and milk. Return pan to heat. Bring slowly to a boil, stirring or whisking, then continue to cook until mixture thickens. Simmer 3 minutes. Stir olives and dill into sauce.

Stir in fennel puree and season with salt and pepper, mixing together well. Reheat sauce gently and adjust seasoning before serving. Serve with fish or poultry.

Makes 3-1/4 cups/52 tablespoons.

Calories per tablespoon: 10
Fat per tablespoon: 0.5 g

—RATATOUILLE PASTA SAUCE—

1 onion
2 garlic cloves
1 tablespoon olive oil
1 eggplant
3 zucchini
1 green bell pepper
1 red bell pepper
1 (14-1/2-oz.) can crushed tomatoes
1 (8-oz.) can crushed tomatoes
1 tablespoon tomato paste
1 teaspoon dried basil
1 teaspoon dried oregano
Salt and pepper

Slice onion and crush both garlic cloves.

In a large saucepan, heat oil 1 minute. Cook onion and garlic 3 minutes, stirring. Dice eggplant, slice zucchini, and slice bell peppers, then add to saucepan.

Stir in tomatoes, tomato paste, herbs, salt, and pepper and mix together well. Bring slowly to a boil, then cover and simmer 30 minutes, stirring occasionally. Adjust seasoning before serving. Serve with freshly cooked pasta.

Makes 4 servings.

Calories per serving: 127
Fat per serving: 5.0 g

—SMOKED HAM & LEEK SAUCE—

8 ounces leeks, well washed
2 tablespoons low-fat margarine
1/4 cup all-purpose flour
1-3/4 cups low-fat milk
6 ounces cooked smoked ham
1 tablespoon snipped fresh chives
3/4 cup grated reduced-fat cheddar cheese
Salt and pepper

Using a sharp knife, chop leeks finely. In a saucepan over low heat, melt margarine. Add leeks and cook 8 to 10 minutes or until soft, stirring.

Stir in flour and cook 1 minute, stirring. Remove pan from heat and gradually stir in milk. Bring slowly to a boil, stirring, then continue to cook until mixture thickens. Simmer 3 minutes. Remove pan from heat.

Chop ham finely and add to sauce with chives. Stir in cheese, salt, and pepper and mix together well. Reheat sauce gently, stirring, but do not let sauce boil. Serve with vegetables, such as squash, potatoes, or broccoli.

Makes 3-1/2 cups/56 tablespoons.

Calories per tablespoon: 15
Fat per tablespoon: 0.7 g

Variation: This is a very thick sauce; add extra liquid if a thinner sauce is preferred.

—BOLOGNESE PASTA SAUCE—

1 onion
1 garlic clove
1 tablespoon sunflower oil
2 carrots
2 stalks celery
8 ounces mushrooms
2 ounces lean bacon, diced
1 pound extra-lean ground beef
1 (14-1/2-oz.) can crushed tomatoes
1 tablespoon tomato paste
2/3 cup beef stock
2/3 cup dry white wine
1 teaspoon Italian seasoning
1/4 teaspoon ground bay leaves or fresh bay leaves
Salt and pepper

Chop onion and crush garlic. In a large sauce-pan, heat oil 1 minute. Add onion and garlic and cook 3 minutes, stirring. Using a sharp knife, finely chop carrots and celery and slice mushrooms. Add to saucepan and cook 5 minutes, stirring. Add bacon and ground beef to saucepan, mixing together well. Cook until meat is browned all over, stirring.

Stir in tomatoes, tomato paste, stock, wine, herbs, salt, and pepper and mix together well. Bring slowly to a boil, then cover and simmer 1-1/2 to 2 hours, stirring occasion-ally. Uncover last 30 minutes of cooking time. Adjust seasoning before serving. Serve with freshly cooked spaghetti or pasta shapes.

Makes 6 servings.

Calories per serving: 207
Fat per serving: 9.5 g

SEAFOOD SAUCE

1 small leek, well washed
2 garlic cloves
2 teaspoons olive oil
2 large tomatoes
2/3 cup fish stock
2/3 cup dry sherry
Salt and pepper
16 cooked mussels, shelled
4 ounces cooked shelled shrimp
6 shucked oysters
1 (6-oz.) can crabmeat, drained
1 tablespoons cornstarch

Slice leek and crush garlic.

In a saucepan, heat oil 1 minute. Add leek and garlic and cook 5 minutes, stirring. Peel and chop tomatoes and add to saucepan. Stir in stock, sherry, salt, and pepper and mix together well. Bring slowly to a boil, then cover and simmer 15 to 20 minutes, stirring occasionally. Stir in seafood. In a small bowl, blend cornstarch with 1 tablespoon cold water.

Stir cornstarch mixture into sauce and bring slowly to a boil, stirring, until sauce thickens. Simmer 3 minutes. Remove pan from heat and adjust seasoning before serving. Serve with pasta, boiled rice, or a selection of vegetables.

Makes 4 cups/64 tablespoons.

Calories per tablespoon: 14
Fat per tablespoon: 0.3 g

SHELLFISH PASTA SAUCE

1 bunch green onions
2 garlic cloves
6 ounces button mushrooms
2 teaspoons olive oil
8 ounces shelled cooked mussels
8 ounces shelled cooked clams
8 ounces shelled cooked fresh scallops
1 (14-1/2-oz) can crushed tomatoes
2/3 cup dry white wine
Finely grated zest of 1/2 lemon
Salt and pepper
2 tablespoons chopped fresh parsley

Coarsely chop green onions and crush garlic. Halve mushrooms, if preferred.

In a large saucepan, heat oil 1 minute. Add onions, garlic, and mushrooms and cook 5 minutes, stirring. Add shellfish to the pan. Stir in tomatoes, wine, lemon zest, salt, and pepper, mixing together well. Bring slowly to a boil, then cover and simmer 5 to 10 minutes, stirring occasionally.

Stir parsley into sauce. Adjust seasoning before serving. Serve with freshly cooked pasta.

Makes 4 servings.

Calories per serving: 253
Fat per serving: 5.4 g

Variation: Use any combination of shellfish for this sauce.

——— SMOKED FISH SAUCE ———

12 ounces skinned smoked haddock fillets
1-1/4 cups low-fat milk
1 shallot
2 tablespoons low-fat margarine
1/4 cup all-purpose flour
1/2 cup low-fat cream cheese
1 tablespoon chopped fresh tarragon
Salt and pepper

Place fish into a saucepan and add milk. Bring milk slowly to a boil, then cover and simmer 15 minutes or until fish is cooked through and flakes easily.

Strain fish, reserving milk. Flake fish. Chop shallot finely. In a saucepan over low heat, melt margarine. Add shallot and cook 5 minutes, stirring. Stir or whisk in flour and cook 1 minute, stirring. Remove pan from heat and gradually stir or whisk in reserved milk. Bring slowly to a boil, stirring or whisking, then continue to cook until mixture thickens. Simmer 3 minutes. Remove pan from heat and stir in fish and cream cheese, mixing together well.

Stir tarragon into sauce and season with salt and pepper. Reheat sauce gently and adjust seasoning before serving. Serve with vegetable dishes or eggs and slices of toast.

Makes 2-3/4 cups/44 tablespoons.

Calories per tablespoon: 19
Fat per tablespoon: 0.8 g

Variation: Use other types of smoked fish, such as smoked mackerel, in place of smoked haddock, if you like.

TUNA SAUCE

1 (6-1/8-oz.) can tuna packed in water
1/2 cup low-fat cream cheese
2/3 cup low-fat plain yogurt
1 tablespoon lemon juice
2 tablespoons chopped fresh parsley
Salt and pepper

Drain and flake tuna into a bowl.

Stir cream cheese, plain yogurt, lemon juice, parsley, salt, and pepper into tuna and mix together well. Cover and refrigerate 30 minutes before serving to let flavors blend.

Serve with cold cooked chicken, hard-cooked eggs, rice, or pasta.

Makes 1-3/4 cups/28 tablespoons.

Calories per tablespoon: 17
Fat per tablespoon: 0.7 g

OYSTER SAUCE

2 tablespoons low-fat margarine
1/4 cup all-purpose flour
1-1/4 cups fish stock
10 oysters in shells
1 tablespoon chopped fresh parsley
Finely grated zest of 1/2 lemon
Salt and pepper

In a saucepan over low heat, melt margarine. Stir in flour and cook 1 minute, stirring. Remove pan from heat and gradually whisk in fish stock. Bring slowly to a boil, whisking, then continue to boil until mixture thickens.

Simmer 3 minutes, then remove pan from heat. Open oysters, remove from shells, and coarsely chop.

Stir oysters, parsley, lemon zest, salt, and pepper into sauce and reheat gently. Adjust seasoning before serving. Serve with fish, pasta, or rice.

Makes 1-1/4 cups/20 tablespoons.

Calories per tablespoon: 15
Fat per tablespoon: 0.6 g

Variation: Substitute canned oysters, drained, for fresh oysters, if desired.

—SALMON & ZUCCHINI SAUCE—

1 small onion
1 small zucchini
2 tablespoons low-fat margarine
1/4 cup all-purpose flour
1-1/4 cups low-fat milk
2/3 cup fish stock
1 (7-1/2-oz.) can red salmon
1 teaspoon dried tarragon
1/4 teaspoon grated nutmeg
Few drops hot-pepper sauce
Salt and pepper

Using a sharp knife, finely chop onion and zucchini. In a saucepan over low heat, melt margarine.

Add onion and zucchini and cook 8 to 10 minutes or until soft, stirring. Stir in flour and cook 1 minute, stirring. Remove pan from heat and gradually stir in milk and stock. Bring slowly to a boil, stirring, then continue to cook until mixture thickens. Simmer 3 minutes.

Drain, bone, and flake salmon, then stir into sauce with tarragon, nutmeg, hot-pepper sauce, salt, and pepper, mixing together well. Reheat sauce gently and adjust seasoning before serving. Serve with pasta, rice, or baked potatoes.

Makes 3 cups/48 tablespoons.

Calories per tablespoon: 16
Fat per tablespoon: 0.8 g

ANCHOVY SAUCE

1 (2-oz.) can anchovy fillets
1 tablespoon margarine
2 tablespoons all-purpose flour
1-1/4 cups low-fat milk
1 tablespoon lemon juice
Salt and pepper

Using a sharp knife, finely chop anchovies and set aside. In a saucepan over low heat, melt margarine. Stir in flour and cook 1 minute, stirring. Remove pan from heat and gradually stir or whisk in milk.

Return pan to heat. Bring slowly to a boil, stirring or whisking, then continue to cook until mixture thickens. Simmer 3 minutes.

Add anchovies to sauce along with lemon juice, salt, and pepper, mixing together well. Reheat sauce gently and adjust seasoning before serving. Serve with fish or shellfish.

Makes 1-1/2 cups/24 tablespoons.

Calories per tablespoon: 23
Fat per tablespoon: 1.6 g

CRANBERRY SAUCE

8 ounces cranberries
1/2 cup sugar
1/4 cup ruby port wine

Place cranberries into a saucepan with 2/3 cup water.

Bring to a boil and boil rapidly until cranberries are soft. Reduce heat and stir in sugar.

Heat gently until sugar dissolves, then stir in port wine. Reheat gently and serve with turkey or pork.

Makes 1-3/4 cups/28 tablespoons.

Calories per tablespoon: 19
Fat per tablespoon: 0 g

Variation: Substitute medium-dry sherry for ruby port wine.

Calories per tablespoon: 19
Fat per tablespoon: 0 g

AVOCADO SAUCE

2 ripe avocado
2/3 cup low-fat plain yogurt
2/3 cup nonfat mayonnaise
1 teaspoon finely grated lemon zest
Juice of 1 lemon
1 tablespoon chopped fresh parsley
Salt and pepper

Using a sharp knife, peel, seed, and coarsely chop avocados.

Into a blender or food processor, put avocados, yogurt, mayonnaise, lemon zest, lemon juice, parsley, salt, and pepper. Blend mixture until it is smooth. Put sauce into a serving dish and adjust seasoning.

Cover and refrigerate 30 minutes before serving to let flavors blend. Serve with fish, poultry, or a low-fat cheese and tomato salad.

Makes 2-1/2 cups/40 tablespoons.

Calories per tablespoon: 26
Fat per tablespoon: 2.5 g

— PINEAPPLE-CHUTNEY SAUCE —

2 garlic cloves
1 (8-oz.) can sliced pineapple packed in fruit juice
1 (8-oz.) can crushed tomatoes
3 tablespoons cider vinegar
2 tablespoons light brown sugar
2 tablespoons mango chutney
2 teaspoons Worcestershire sauce
1/2 teaspoon Dijon mustard
1/2 teaspoon apple pie spice
Few drops hot-pepper sauce
Salt and pepper
1 tablespoon cornstarch

Crush garlic and coarsely chop pineapple.

Combine garlic, pineapple, tomatoes, vinegar, sugar, chutney, Worcestershire sauce, mustard, apple pie spice, hot-pepper sauce, salt, and pepper in a saucepan. Bring slowly to a boil, then cover and simmer 10 minutes, stirring occasionally. Remove pan from heat and set aside to cool. When slightly cool, in a blender or food processor, puree mixture until smooth. Return sauce to clean saucepan.

In a small bowl, blend cornstarch with 1 tablespoon water. Stir cornstarch mixture into sauce and bring slowly to a boil, stirring constantly. Simmer 3 minutes, stirring occasionally and adjust seasoning before serving. Serve with grilled or broiled meats, such as steaks, chops, or chicken.

Makes 1-3/4 cups/28 tablespoons.

Calories per tablespoon: 14
Fat per tablespoon: 0.1 g

SPICED APPLESAUCE

1 pound cooking apples
1 small onion
2 tablespoons low-fat margarine
2 tablespoons light brown sugar
1 teaspoon apple pie spice

Peel, core, and thinly slice apples. Finely chop onion. Put apples into a saucepan and add 2 tablespoons water. Cover saucepan and cook apples over low heat until apples are soft, stirring occasionally.

Remove pan from heat and mash apples thoroughly with a fork or potato masher. In a separate saucepan over low heat, melt margarine. Add onion and cook 8 to 10 minutes or until soft, stirring occasionally.

Stir in mashed apples, sugar, and apple pie spice, mixing together well. Simmer until sugar dissolves. Serve hot or cold with pork, ham, or goose.

Makes 2-1/2 cups/40 tablespoons.

Calories per tablespoon: 8
Fat per tablespoon: 0.3 g

——— CUMBERLAND SAUCE ———

Finely grated zest and juice of 1 orange
Finely grated zest and juice of 1 lemon
1/4 cup red currant jelly
2 tablespoons red-wine vinegar
1 teaspoon Dijon mustard
Salt and pepper
1 tablespoon cornstarch
1/4 cup ruby port wine

In a saucepan, combine orange zest and juice, lemon zest and juice, red currant jelly, red-wine vinegar, mustard, salt, pepper, and 1/4 cup water.

Bring slowly to a boil, stirring. Cover and simmer 5 minutes, stirring occasionally. In a small bowl, blend cornstarch with 1 tablespoon water and port wine. Stir cornstarch mixture into sauce, mixing together well.

Bring slowly to a boil, stirring constantly, until mixture thickens. Simmer 3 minutes. Remove pan from heat and adjust seasoning before serving. Serve hot or cold with ham, pork, game, or variety meats.

Makes 2 cups/32 tablespoons.

Calories per tablespoon: 10
Fat per tablespoon: 0.01 g

GOOSEBERRY SAUCE

1 pound gooseberries
Finely grated zest and juice of 1 orange
2 tablespoons low-fat margarine
2 tablespoons light brown sugar
1/4 teaspoon grated nutmeg

Place gooseberries into a saucepan. Add orange zest and juice and 2/3 cup water, mixing together well. Bring the mixture slowly to a boil, then reduce heat, cover saucepan, and simmer 5 to 10 minutes or until gooseberries are soft, stirring occasionally.

Remove pan from heat and set aside to cool. When slightly cool, in a blender or food processor, puree gooseberries until smooth. Return mixture to clean saucepan.

Stir in margarine, sugar, and nutmeg. Bring slowly to a boil, stirring, then simmer 1 minute. Serve with oily fish such as mackerel.

Makes 2 cups/32 tablespoons.

Calories per tablespoon: 9
Fat per tablespoon: 0.4 g

SWEET & SOUR SAUCE

8 ounces carrots
6 green onions
1 garlic clove
1 (1-inch) piece gingerroot
2 teaspoons olive oil
1 cup unsweetened applesauce
2 cups beef stock
2/3 cup red wine
3 tablespoons lemon juice
2 tablespoons honey
2 tablespoons soy sauce
Salt and pepper
1 tablespoon cornstarch

Grate carrots coarsely and finely chop green onions. Crush garlic. Peel and grate ginger or finely chop. In a saucepan, heat oil 1 minute. Add carrots, green onions, garlic, and ginger root and cook 5 minutes, stirring. Stir in applesauce, stock, wine, lemon juice, honey, soy sauce, salt, and pepper and mix together well. Bring slowly to a boil, then cover and simmer 1 hour, stirring occasionally. Remove pan from heat and press the sauce through a nylon strainer. Discard pulp and return sauce to clean saucepan.

In a small bowl, blend cornstarch with 1 tablespoon water. Stir cornstarch mixture into sauce and bring slowly to a boil, stirring constantly. Simmer 3 minutes and adjust seasoning before serving. Serve with lamb, pork, fresh vegetables, or mixed beans.

Makes 2-3/4 cups/44 tablespoons.

Calories per tablespoon: 12
Fat per tablespoon: 0.3 g

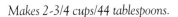

RHUBARB SAUCE

1 pound rhubarb
8 ounces cooking apples
1/2 cup sugar
2 tablespoons low-fat margarine

Using a sharp knife, trim rhubarb and cut into 1-inch slices. Peel, core, and thinly slice apples.

Place rhubarb and apples into a saucepan and add 2/3 cup water. Bring slowly to a boil, then reduce heat, cover, and simmer until fruit is soft and pulpy, stirring occasionally. Remove pan from heat and mash fruit thoroughly with a fork or potato masher.

Stir sugar and margarine into mashed rhubarb and apples and mix together well. Bring slowly to a boil, then simmer 1 minute, stirring. Serve sauce hot or cold with oily fish, such as mackerel.

Makes 3-1/2 cups/56 tablespoons.

Calories per tablespoon: 12
Fat per tablespoon: 0.2 g

FIG SAUCE

2 shallots or 1 onion
8 ounces dried figs
2 teaspoons olive oil
1-1/4 cups chicken stock
2 tablespoons cider vinegar
1 tablespoon chopped fresh thyme
Salt and pepper

Using a sharp knife, finely chop shallots or onion and coarsely chop figs. In a saucepan, heat oil 1 minute. Add shallots or onion and figs and cook 5 minutes, stirring.

Stir in stock, vinegar, thyme, salt, and pepper and mix together well. Bring slowly to a boil, then reduce heat, cover, and simmer 10 minutes, stirring occasionally. Remove pan from heat and set aside to cool.

When slightly cool, in a blender or food processor, puree mixture until smooth. Return sauce to clean saucepan. Reheat gently and adjust seasoning before serving. Serve hot or cold with lamb or beef.

Makes 2 cups/32 tablespoons.

Calories per tablespoon: 18
Fat per tablespoon: 0.4 g

PLUM SAUCE

12 ounces red dessert plums
Finely grated zest and juice of 1 orange
1/4 cup sugar
1/2 teaspoon ground cinnamon
1 tablespoon brandy

Halve and pit plums. Place plums into a saucepan and add 2/3 cup cold water.

Bring slowly to a boil, then reduce heat, cover, and simmer until plums are soft, stirring occasionally. Remove pan from heat and set aside to cool. When slightly cool, in a blender or food processor, puree plums and cooking liquid until smooth.

Return sauce to clean saucepan and stir in orange zest, orange juice, sugar, cinnamon, and brandy, mixing together well. Reheat sauce gently before serving or serve sauce cold. Serve with lamb, pork, or beef.

Makes 2-1/4 cups/36 tablespoons.

Calories per tablespoon: 10
Fat per tablespoon: 0.01 g

– PINEAPPLE & ORANGE SAUCE –

10 ounces fresh pineapple
2 oranges
3 tablespoons apricot jam or preserves
1 teaspoon arrowroot
1 teaspoon apple pie spice (optional)

Using a sharp knife, coarsely chop pineapple. Peel oranges and coarsely chop flesh. Put pineapple, oranges, and jam or preserves into a saucepan and add 2/3 cup water and mix together well. Bring slowly to a boil, stirring. Reduce heat, cover, and simmer 15 minutes, stirring occasionally.

Remove pan from heat and set aside to cool. When slightly cool, in a blender or food processor, puree mixture until smooth. Strain mixture through a nylon strainer, discarding pulp. Return sauce to clean saucepan. In a small bowl, blend arrowroot with 1 tablespoon water.

Stir arrowroot mixture into sauce. Bring slowly to a boil, stirring constantly until sauce thickens. Stir in apple pie spice, if using, before serving. Serve hot with chicken or turkey, or serve cold with low-fat or nonfat frozen yogurt.

Makes 2 cups/32 tablespoons.

Calories per tablespoon: 12
Fat per tablespoon: 0.03 g

MELON & GINGER SAUCE

1 cantaloupe melon
3 ounces preserved stem ginger
2/3 cup low-fat plain yogurt
2 tablespoons syrup from ginger
1 tablespoon ginger wine or sweet sherry

Using a sharp knife, peel and seed melon and coarsely chop flesh. Into a blender or food processor, place melon and blend until smooth.

Pour pureed melon into a bowl. Chop ginger finely, then stir into melon, mixing together well. Stir in yogurt, ginger syrup, and wine and mix together well.

Cover and refrigerate sauce at least 30 minutes before serving to let flavors blend. Serve with fruit-flavored gelatin or fresh fruit.

Makes 2-3/4 cups/44 tablespoons.

Calories per tablespoon: 9
Fat per tablespoon: 0.06 g

Variation: Use another type of melon such as galia, ogen, or honeydew.

───── THICK FRUIT SAUCE ─────

4 ounces plums
4 ounces raspberries
4 ounces strawberries
4 ounces blackberries
1 cup sugar
Juice of 1 lime
2 teaspoons arrowroot

Halve and pit plums. Put plums, raspberries, strawberries, and blackberries into a saucepan and add 2/3 cup water.

Bring slowly to a boil, then reduce heat, cover, and simmer until fruit is soft, stirring occasionally. Remove pan from heat and set aside to cool. When slightly cool, in a blender or food processor, puree fruit until smooth. Return sauce to clean saucepan. Stir in sugar and lime juice and mix together well. Return pan to heat. In a small bowl, blend arrowroot with 1 tablespoon water.

Stir arrowroot mixture into sauce. Bring slowly to a boil, stirring constantly, until sauce thickens. Serve hot or cold with low-fat on nonfat frozen yogurt.

Makes 3 cups/48 tablespoons.

Calories per tablespoon: 13
Fat per tablespoon: 0.01 g

Variation: Use any mixture of fruit you like.

FRUITY YOGURT SAUCE

1 (11-oz.) can mandarin orange segments packed in
  fruit juice
1 (8-oz.) can pineapple slices packed in fruit juice
1-1/4 cups low-fat plain yogurt
1/2 cup powdered sugar

Into a blender or food processor, put oranges
and pineapple and their juices. Puree until
smooth.

Pour pureed fruit into a bowl. Stir in yogurt
and mix together well. Sift powdered sugar
into a bowl.

Gently fold powdered sugar into fruit sauce,
mixing together well. Cover and refrigerate
30 minutes before serving to let flavors blend.
Serve with fresh fruit or baked desserts.

Makes 3-3/4 cups/60 tablespoons.

Calories per tablespoon: 10
Fat per tablespoon: 0.04 g

Variation: Use other canned fruits in fruit
juices for a different flavored sauce.

-RASPBERRY & ALMOND SAUCE-

8 ounces raspberries
1/4 cup sugar
2/3 cup medium-dry white wine
1 teaspoon arrowroot
Few drops almond extract

Put raspberries into a saucepan and add 2 tablespoons water. Bring slowly to a boil, then cover and simmer until raspberries are soft, stirring occasionally. Remove pan from heat and set aside to cool. When slightly cool, in a blender or food processor, puree raspberries until smooth.

Press raspberry puree through a nylon strainer and discard seeds. Return sauce to clean saucepan and stir in sugar and wine, mixing together well. Return pan to heat. In a small bowl, blend arrowroot with 1 tablespoon water.

Stir arrowroot mixture into sauce. Bring slowly to a boil, stirring constantly, until sauce thickens. Stir in a few drops of almond extract before serving. Serve hot or cold with baked desserts, low-fat or nonfat frozen yogurt, or fresh fruit.

Makes 1-1/4 cups/20 tablespoons.

Calories per tablespoon: 20
Fat per tablespoon: 0.03 g

— PEAR & RASPBERRY SAUCE —

8 ounces raspberries
1 (16-oz.) can pear halves packed in fruit juice
1/4 cup sugar
2 tablespoons brandy
1 teaspoon arrowroot

Into a blender or food processor, put raspberries, pears, and pear juice. Puree fruit until smooth.

Press fruit puree through a nylon strainer into a saucepan and discard seeds. Stir in sugar and brandy and mix together well.

In a small bowl, blend arrowroot with 1 tablespoon water, then stir into sauce. Bring slowly to a boil, stirring constantly, until sauce thickens. Serve hot or cold with mousses, crepes, or a steamed pudding.

Makes 2-1/4 cups/36 tablespoons.

Calories per tablespoon: 13
Fat per tablespoon: 0.02 g

Variation: Substitute peaches or pineapple packed in fruit juice for pears.

SATSUMA SAUCE

10 satsumas (mandarin oranges)
1 tablespoon lemon juice
1/3 cup light brown sugar
2 teaspoons arrowroot
5 teaspoons Cointreau or other orange liqueur

Peel and segment satsumas. Put satsumas and lemon juice into a saucepan and add 2/3 cup water. Cover and simmer until satsumas are soft, stirring occasionally.

Remove pan from heat and set aside to cool. When slightly cool, in a blender or food processor, puree mixture until smooth. Pour pureed satsumas into a saucepan, add sugar, and mix together well. Heat mixture gently until sugar dissolves, stirring. In a small bowl, blend arrowroot with 1 tablespoon water until smooth. Stir arrowroot mixture into fruit, mixing together well.

Reheat gently until sauce thickens, stirring constantly. Stir in Cointreau or other orange liqueur and mix together well. Serve with baked desserts or low-fat cheesecakes.

Makes 2-1/4 cups/36 tablespoons.

Calories per tablespoon: 13
Fat per tablespoon: 0.02 g

Variation: Once fruit has been pureed, strain puree through a nylon strainer, if preferred.

CHOCOLATE SAUCE

1 tablespoon unsweetened cocoa powder
2 tablespoons sugar
1 tablespoon cornstarch
1-1/4 cups low-fat milk
1 tablespoon low-fat margarine

Sift cocoa powder into a bowl. Add sugar, cornstarch, and a little of the milk, blending until smooth.

Add remaining milk and margarine to a saucepan and bring slowly to a boil. Remove pan from heat and pour hot milk onto blended cocoa mixture, whisking.

Return sauce to saucepan and reheat gently, stirring constantly, until sauce thickens. Simmer 3 minutes. Serve with custards, puddings, and profiteroles filled with low-fat custard or fresh fruit.

Makes 1-1/4 cups/20 tablespoons.

Calories per tablespoon: 21
Fat per tablespoon: 0.7 g

BRANDY SAUCE

2 tablespoons cornstarch
1-1/4 cups low-fat milk
2 tablespoons sugar
3 tablespoons brandy

In a bowl, blend cornstarch with 2 table-spoons milk until smooth. Into a saucepan, put remaining milk and bring slowly to a boil.

Pour hot milk onto cornstarch mixture, whisking. Return sauce to saucepan and bring slowly to a boil, stirring constantly, until sauce thickens. Simmer 3 minutes.

Remove pan from heat and stir in sugar and brandy. Reheat sauce gently. Serve with plum pudding or apple tartlets.

Makes 1-1/4 cups/20 tablespoons.

Calories per tablespoon: 23
Fat per tablespoon: 0.3 g

Variation: Replace brandy with rum, sherry, or whiskey.

CARAMEL SAUCE

3/4 cup light brown sugar
1/2 cup sugar
1 tablespoon arrowroot

Into a saucepan, put sugars with 2 cups water. Heat mixture gently until sugar dissolves. Bring slowly to a boil, then simmer 10 minutes, stirring occasionally.

In a small bowl, blend arrowroot with 2 tablespoons water. Whisk arrowroot mixture into sugar mixture, mixing together well. Reheat sauce gently, until sauce thickens, stirring constantly.

Serve with fruit such as oranges or bananas.

Makes 1-3/4 cups/28 tablespoons.

Calories per tablespoon: 34
Fat per tablespoon: 0 g

Variation: Once sauce has thickened, add 2 to 3 tablespoons brandy or a liqueur such as Cointreau to sauce and reheat gently.

Calories per tablespoon: 38
Fat per tablespoon: 0 g

CUSTARD SAUCE

1 tablespoon superfine sugar
1 tablespoon cornstarch
Pinch of salt
2 egg yolks
1-1/4 cups low-fat milk
Few drops vanilla extract

Into a heatproof bowl, put sugar, cornstarch, salt, and egg yolks. Add 2 tablespoons of the milk and whisk until smooth. In a saucepan, bring remaining milk slowly to a boil.

Pour hot milk onto cornstarch mixture, whisking together well. Return mixture to saucepan and bring slowly to a boil, whisking constantly, until mixture thickens and coats back of spoon.

Simmer 1 minute. Whisk in a few drops of vanilla extract before serving. Serve with baked apples or canned or fresh fruit.

Makes 1-1/4 cups/20 tablespoons.

Calories per tablespoon: 19
Fat per tablespoon: 0.9g

MELBA SAUCE

1 pound raspberries
1 cup powdered sugar
3 tablespoons medium-dry white wine
1 teaspoon arrowroot

Into a saucepan, put raspberries with 2 table-spoons water. Cover and cook raspberries gently until they are soft. Remove pan from heat and set aside to cool.

When slightly cool, strain raspberries through a nylon strainer, discarding seeds. Sift powdered sugar, then place in saucepan with raspberry sauce and wine, mixing together well. Heat sauce gently until sugar dissolves, then bring to a boil. Remove pan from heat. In a small bowl, blend arrowroot with 1 tablespoon water.

Stir arrowroot mixture into raspberry sauce. Reheat gently until sauce thickens, stirring constantly. Serve hot or cold with peaches, low-fat ice cream, or sorbet.

Makes 2-1/4 cups/36 tablespoons.

Calories per tablespoon: 18
Fat per tablespoon: 0.04 g

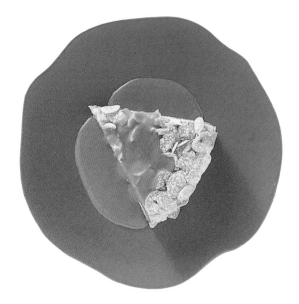

COFFEE SAUCE

4 teaspoons cornstarch
1-1/4 cups low-fat milk
2 teaspoons instant coffee granules
2 tablespoons sugar

In a heatproof bowl, blend cornstarch with 2 tablespoons milk until smooth. In a saucepan, bring remaining milk slowly to a boil.

Pour hot milk onto cornstarch mixture, stirring. Return sauce to clean saucepan and bring slowly to a boil, stirring constantly, until mixture thickens. Simmer 3 minutes. Remove pan from heat. In a small bowl, dissolve coffee in 2 tablespoons hot water.

Stir coffee and sugar into sauce, then reheat gently before serving. Serve with stewed fruit, frozen yogurt, or low-calorie pies.

Makes 1-2/3 cups/26 tablespoons.

Calories per tablespoon: 13
Fat per tablespoon: 0.2 g

APRICOT SAUCE

8 ounces dried apricots
1/4 cup sugar
1-1/4 cups dry white wine

Chop apricots roughly. Into a saucepan, place sugar with 2/3 cup water. Heat mixture gently until sugar dissolves.

Stir in apricots and wine, mixing together well. Bring slowly to a boil, then cover and simmer 20 minutes, stirring occasionally. Remove pan from heat and set aside to cool.

When slightly cool, in a blender or food processor, puree mixture until smooth. Return sauce to saucepan and reheat gently before serving. Serve with baked desserts, crepes, or baked fruit, such as baked pears.

Makes 2-1/4 cups/36 tablespoons.

Calories per tablespoon: 21
Fat per tablespoon: 0.04 g

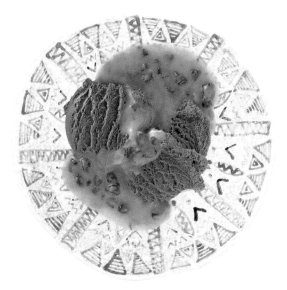

RUM & RAISIN SAUCE

3 tablespoons cornstarch
5 teaspoons sugar
2 cups low-fat milk
1/2 cup raisins
1/4 cup rum
2 tablespoons reduced-fat light cream

In a heatproof bowl or jug, blend cornstarch and sugar with 2 tablespoons milk until smooth. In a saucepan, bring remaining milk slowly to a boil. Pour hot milk onto cornstarch mixture, stirring, then return mixture to saucepan.

Reheat gently until sauce thickens, stirring constantly. Simmer 3 minutes, then remove pan from heat. Chop raisins roughly and stir into sauce.

Stir in rum and cream. Reheat sauce very gently, but do not let sauce boil. Serve with crepes or low-fat ice cream.

Makes 2-1/4 cups/36 tablespoons.

Calories per tablespoon: 22
Fat per tablespoon: 0.3 g

LEMON SAUCE

1-1/4 cups low-fat plain yogurt
1/4 cup low-fat cream cheese
1/2 cup powdered sugar
Finely grated zest and juice of 2 lemons

In a bowl, whisk together yogurt and cream cheese. Sift powdered sugar, then stir into yogurt mixture, mixing together well.

Stir in lemon zest and lemon juice and whisk together thoroughly. Cover and leave sauce in a cool place 30 minutes before serving to let flavors develop.

Serve with steamed puddings or fresh fruit compote.

Makes 2 cups/32 tablespoons.

Calories per tablespoon: 18
Fat per tablespoon: 0.6 g

Variation: Use finely grated zest and juice of 2 small oranges in place of lemons. You could also use a mixture of fruit, such as 1 lemon and 1 orange, or 1 lemon and 1 lime.

——RASPBERRY & FIG SAUCE——

8 ounces dried figs
1 (14-oz.) can raspberries packed in light syrup
1/4 cup sugar
2 tablespoons brandy or raspberry liqueur

Using a sharp knife, chop figs roughly. Into a bowl, put figs, raspberries, and juice with 2/3 cup water. Mix together well. Cover and leave to soak in a cool place overnight.

In a blender or food processor, puree fruit mixture until smooth.

Into a saucepan, put puree. Stir in sugar and brandy or liqueur. Bring slowly to a boil, then simmer 1 minute. Serve with mousses, molded desserts, baked deserts, or crepes.

Makes 3 cups/48 tablespoons.

Calories per tablespoon: 25
Fat per tablespoon: 0.09 g

Note: Once the fruit has been pureed, strain it through a nylon strainer to remove seeds, if preferred.

——— SWEET SHERRY SAUCE ———

5 teaspoons cornstarch
1-1/4 cups low-fat milk
5 teaspoons sugar
3 tablespoons sweet sherry

In a heatproof bowl, blend cornstarch with 2 tablespoons milk until smooth. In a saucepan, bring remaining milk slowly to a boil.

Remove pan from heat and pour hot milk onto cornstarch mixture, stirring constantly. Return mixture to saucepan and reheat gently until mixture thickens, stirring constantly.

Remove pan from heat and stir in sugar and sherry, mixing together well. Reheat sauce gently before serving. Serve with steamed or baked fruit desserts.

Makes 1-1/2 cups/23 tablespoons.

Calories per tablespoon: 17
Fat per tablespoon: 0.2 g

—BLACKBERRY & APPLE SAUCE—

8 ounces cooking apples
8 ounces blackberries
1/4 cup sugar
1/2 cup low-fat cream cheese
2/3 cup reduced-fat light cream

Using a sharp knife, peel, core, and slice apples thinly. Into a saucepan, put apples and blackberries along with 3 tablespoons water. Cover and cook gently until fruit is soft, stirring occasionally.

Remove pan from heat and stir in sugar. Set aside to cool. When slightly cool, in a blender or food processor, puree fruit until smooth. Press fruit through a nylon strainer, discarding seeds.

Beat cream cheese and cream together, then whisk fruit in, mixing together thoroughly. Serve with steamed and baked puddings, meringues, or poached fruit such as peaches or pears.

Makes 2-1/4 cups/36 tablespoons.

Calories per tablespoon: 20
Fat per tablespoon: 0.9 g

Variation: In place of blackberries, use raspberries, loganberries, or black currants.

MADEIRA SAUCE

3/4 cup light brown sugar
3 tablespoons brandy
1/4 cup low-fat margarine
2/3 cup Madeira wine
1 tablespoon arrowroot

Into a saucepan, put sugar and brandy along with 1-1/4 cups water. Heat gently, stirring, until sugar dissolves.

Stir in margarine and Madeira wine, then bring slowly to a boil, whisking constantly. Remove pan from heat. In a small bowl, blend arrowroot with 2 tablespoons water until smooth.

Stir arrowroot mixture into sauce, mixing together well. Reheat sauce gently, stirring constantly, until sauce thickens. Serve with steamed or baked fruit puddings or low-fat ice cream.

Makes 3-1/4 cups/52 tablespoons.

Calories per tablespoon: 20
Fat per tablespoon: 0.4 g

MANGO SAUCE

1 mango
3 tablespoons low-fat margarine
1/2 cup all-purpose flour
2 cups low-fat milk
1/3 cup light brown sugar

Peel and pit mango, then chop flesh roughly. Place mango in a blender or food processor and puree until smooth. Set aside. In a saucepan over low heat, melt margarine. Stir in flour and cook 1 minute, stirring.

Remove pan from heat and gradually whisk in milk. Return pan to heat. Bring slowly to a boil, whisking, then continue to cook until mixture thickens. Simmer 3 minutes.

Remove pan from heat and stir in pureed mango along with sugar, mixing together well. Reheat sauce gently before serving. Serve with a fresh tropical fruit salad or fruit compote.

Makes 2-3/4 cups/44 tablespoons.

Calories per tablespoon: 20
Fat per tablespoon: 0.6 g

GINGER SAUCE

1/4 cup sugar
2 ounces preserved stem ginger
1/4 cup syrup from ginger
2 tablespoons lemon juice
1 teaspoon arrowroot

Into a saucepan, put sugar with 2/3 cup water. Heat gently until sugar dissolves, stirring, then bring to a boil and boil 5 minutes.

Chop ginger finely, then stir into sugar mixture with ginger syrup and lemon juice, mixing together well. In a small bowl, blend arrowroot with 1 tablespoon water until smooth.

Stir arrowroot mixture into sauce. Reheat gently, stirring constantly, until sauce thickens. Serve with fresh melon, a fresh fruit salad, or hot steamed puddings.

Makes 1 cup/16 tablespoons.

Calories per tablespoon: 29
Fat per tablespoon: 0.02 g

MIXED BERRY SAUCE

4 ounces raspberries
4 ounces blackberries
4 ounces gooseberries
3 tablespoons honey
1 teaspoon apple pie spice

Into a saucepan, put raspberries, blackberries, and gooseberries along with 3 tablespoons water. Cover and cook gently until
fruit is soft, stirring occasionally. Remove
pan from heat and set aside to cool.

When slightly cool, in a blender or food processor, puree fruit until smooth. Press fruit
puree through a nylon strainer, then discard
seeds.

Into clean saucepan, put strained puree, then
stir in honey and spice, mixing together well.
Reheat sauce gently, stirring. Serve hot or
cold with crepes, pancakes, summer desserts,
or baked desserts.

Makes 1-1/4 cups/20 tablespoons.

Calories per tablespoon: 10
Fat per tablespoon: 0.06 g

Variation: Use any mixture of fruit of your
choice.

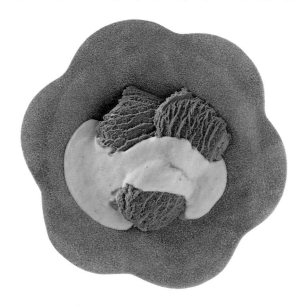

—BANANA & GINGER SAUCE—

3 bananas, about 1 pound in weight
Juice of 1 lemon
Juice of 1 lime
2 cups low-fat plain yogurt
3 tablespoons light brown sugar
2 teaspoons ground ginger

Using a sharp knife, peel and slice bananas.
Into a blender or food processor, put bananas,
lemon juice, and lime juice, and blend until
smooth.

Add yogurt, sugar, and ginger to blender or
food processor and blend mixture until
thoroughly mixed.

Pour sauce into a suitable serving dish. Cover
and leave sauce in a cool place 30 minutes
before serving to let flavors develop. Serve
with fresh fruit, low-fat ice cream, or frozen
yogurt.

Makes 2-3/4 cups/44 tablespoons.

Calories per tablespoon: 17
Fat per tablespoon: 0.1 g

-STRAWBERRY & LEMON SAUCE-

8 ounces strawberries
Finely grated zest and juice of 2 lemons
1/4 cup sugar
1 teaspoon arrowroot

Into a blender or food processor, put strawberries and puree until smooth. Pour into a saucepan.

Into the saucepan, put 2/3 cup water, then stir in lemon zest, lemon juice, and sugar. Heat gently, stirring, until sugar dissolves, then slowly bring mixture to a boil and simmer 5 minutes. In a small bowl, blend arrowroot with 1 tablespoon water until smooth.

Stir arrowroot mixture into saucepan, mixing together well. Reheat sauce gently until mixture thickens, stirring constantly. Serve with fruit gelatin desserts, fresh fruit, fruit tart, or sorbet.

Makes 1-3/4 cups/28 tablespoons.

Calories per tablespoon: 10
Fat per tablespoon: 0.008 g

——VANILLA-YOGURT SAUCE——

2/3 cup low-fat milk
1 vanilla bean
1 teaspoon cornstarch
1/2 cup powdered sugar
1-1/4 cups low-fat plain yogurt

In a saucepan, warm milk. Split vanilla bean lengthwise, then add to milk. Remove pan from heat, cover, and set aside 15 minutes to infuse.

Remove vanilla bean and scrape seeds from bean into milk. In a small bowl, blend cornstarch with 1 tablespoon water until smooth. Stir cornstarch mixture into milk and bring slowly to a boil, stirring constantly, until mixture thickens. Simmer sauce gently 3 minutes, stirring.

Remove pan from heat, pour sauce into a bowl and set aside to cool. Sift powdered sugar into a bowl. Once the cornstarch sauce is cool, stir in the powdered sugar and yogurt and mix together thoroughly. Serve with hot or cold desserts, or meringues.

Makes 1-3/4 cups/28 tablespoons.

Calories per tablespoon: 17
Fat per tablespoon: 0.2 g

BLACK CURRANT SAUCE

8 ounces black currants
3 tablespoons honey
2 tablespoons black currant liqueur, such as cassis
1 teaspoon arrowroot

Remove black currants from strings, then place in a saucepan with honey and 1/4 cup water. Cover and cook mixture gently until black currants are soft, stirring occasionally.

Remove pan from heat and stir in black currant liqueur. In a small bowl, blend arrowroot with 1 tablespoon water until smooth. Stir arrowroot mixture into black currants and mix together well.

Bring slowly to a boil, stirring constantly, until sauce thickens. Serve hot or cold with frozen yogurt or fresh fruit such as figs.

Makes 1-3/4 cups/28 tablespoons.

Calories per tablespoon: 9
Fat per tablespoon: 0 g

—— KIWIFRUIT & LIME SAUCE ——

8 ripe kiwifruit, approximately 1 pound in weight
Finely grated zest and juice of 1 lime
1/2 cup low-fat cream cheese
2/3 cup reduced-fat light cream
1/2 cup powdered sugar

Using a sharp knife, peel and quarter kiwifruit. Put kiwi fruit, lime zest, and lime juice in a blender or food processor and blend until smooth.

Add cream cheese and cream to blender or food processor and blend until thoroughly mixed. Into a bowl, pour sauce.

Sift powdered sugar, then stir into sauce, mixing together well. Cover and leave the sauce to stand in a cool place 30 minutes before serving to let flavors develop. Serve with low-fat ice cream, sorbet, or a fresh fruit salad.

Makes 3 cups/48 tablespoons.

Calories per tablespoon: 17
Fat per tablespoon: 0.7 g

SWEET CHERRY-NUTMEG SAUCE

12 ounces sweet cherries, such as bing
3 tablespoons bramble or blackberry jelly
2/3 cup low-fat plain yogurt
2 teaspoons grated nutmeg

Pit cherries and chop them roughly. Into a saucepan, put cherries with bramble or blackberry jelly and 1/4 cup water.

Cook mixture gently, stirring, until jelly dissolves. Cover and continue cooking gently 10 minutes or until cherries are soft, stirring occasionally. Remove pan from heat, pour mixture into a bowl, and set aside to cool.

When slightly cool, stir in yogurt and nutmeg and mix together thoroughly. Serve with fresh fruit, crepes, or low-fat ice cream.

Makes 1-3/4 cups/28 tablespoons.

Calories per tablespoon: 11
Fat per tablespoon: 0.2 g

Variation: For a richer sauce, replace the yogurt with reduced-fat light cream.

Calories per tablespoon: 15
Fat per tablespoon: 0.6 g

– COCONUT-YOGURT DRESSING –

1-1/4 cups low-fat plain yogurt
3 tablespoons shredded coconut
2 tablespoons honey
Juice of 1 lime

Into a bowl, put yogurt and coconut and mix together well.

Whisk in honey and lime juice, mixing together well. Cover and leave dressing in a cool place 30 minutes before serving to let flavors develop.

Serve with a bean salad or a mixed salad.

Makes 1-2/3 cups/26 tablespoons.

Calories per tablespoon: 31
Fat per tablespoon: 2.2 g

Variation: For a special dressing, add 2 tablespoons coconut liqueur, such as Malibu, to dressing with honey.

Calories per tablespoon: 33
Fat per tablespoon: 2.2 g

TARTAR SAUCE

7 or 8 cornichons (tiny sour pickles)
1 tablespoon capers, drained
1-1/4 cups reduced-calorie mayonnaise
1 tablespoon tarragon vinegar
1 tablespoon chopped fresh parsley
1 tablespoon snipped fresh chives
2 teaspoons chopped fresh tarragon
Salt and pepper

Using a sharp knife, finely chop cornichons
(pickles) and capers.

Into a bowl, put cornichons (pickles) and
capers and stir in mayonnaise, mixing
together well.

Stir in vinegar, parsley, chives, tarragon, and
salt and pepper and mix together thoroughly.
Cover and leave in a cool place at least 30
minutes before serving to let flavors develop.
Serve with grilled, broiled, or baked fish.

Makes 1-2/3 cups/26 tablespoons.

Calories per tablespoon: 34
Fat per tablespoon: 3 g

– THOUSAND ISLAND DRESSING –

1 medium-size dill pickle
2 tablespoons chopped red bell pepper
2 tablespoons chopped green bell pepper
1-1/4 cups reduced-calorie mayonnaise
1/4 cup low-fat plain yogurt
2 tablespoons tomato ketchup
1 tablespoon chopped fresh parsley
Salt and pepper

Using a sharp knife, chop pickle finely. In a bowl, mix together pickle and red and green bell peppers.

Stir in mayonnaise, yogurt, tomato ketchup, parsley, salt, and pepper and mix together thoroughly. Cover and leave in a cool place 30 minutes before serving to let flavors develop.

Serve with a fresh mixed seafood salad.

Makes 2-1/2 cups/44 tablespoons.

Calories per tablespoon: 24
Fat per tablespoon: 2.1 g

Variation: Add 2 cold hard-boiled eggs, mashed or finely chopped, to dressing.

Calories per tablespoon: 29
Fat per tablespoon: 2.5 g

—MILD CURRY MAYONNAISE—

6 green onions
1 tablespoon low-fat margarine
2 tablespoons mango chutney
1 tablespoon mild curry powder
1 tablespoon shredded coconut
1-1/4 cups low-fat or nonfat mayonnaise
2/3 cup low-fat plain yogurt
Salt and pepper

Using a sharp knife, trim and chop green onions finely. In a saucepan over low heat, melt margarine. Add green onions and cook 5 minutes, stirring.

Remove pan from heat and stir in chutney, curry powder, and coconut, mixing together well. Set aside to cool.

When cool, mix with mayonnaise, yogurt, salt, and pepper. Cover and leave the sauce in a cool place 30 minutes before serving to let flavors develop. Serve with potato salad or coleslaw.

Makes 2 cups/32 tablespoons.

Calories per tablespoon: 36
Fat per tablespoon: 3 g

——— HOT CHILE DRESSING ———

1 garlic clove
1/2 red chile
1/4 cup olive oil
6 tablespoons cider vinegar
2/3 cup tomato juice
2 tablespoons tomato ketchup
2 teaspoons Dijon mustard
Few drops hot-pepper sauce
Salt and pepper

Peel and crush garlic. Seed and chop chile finely.

Into a bowl, put garlic, chile, olive oil, vinegar, tomato juice, tomato ketchup, mustard, hot-pepper sauce, salt, and pepper.

Beat all the ingredients together until thoroughly mixed. Adjust seasoning before serving. Serve with a seafood or rice salad.

Makes 1-2/3 cups/26 tablespoons.

Calories per tablespoon: 24
Fat per tablespoon: 2.3 g

Note: Instead of whisking ingredients together in a bowl, put all ingredients in a clean jelly jar, screw top on, and shake until all ingredients are well mixed together.

FRENCH DRESSING

1/4 cup olive oil
1/4 cup white-wine vinegar
1/4 cup tarragon vinegar
2/3 cup white grape juice
2 teaspoons chopped fresh mixed herbs, such as
    parsley, thyme, mint, and rosemary
2 teaspoons whole-grain mustard
Pinch sugar
Salt and pepper

Into a bowl, put olive oil, vinegars, grape juice, herbs, mustard, sugar, salt, and pepper. Beat ingredients together until thoroughly mixed.

Alternatively, put all ingredients in a clean jelly jar. Screw top on jar and shake until ingredients are thoroughly mixed.

Adjust seasoning before serving. Serve with a fresh mixed salad or a selection of raw or cooked vegetables.

Makes 1-1/3 cups/21 tablespoons.

Calories per tablespoon: 31
Fat per tablespoon: 2.9 g

WALNUT DRESSING

1 garlic clove
1/4 cup walnut oil
3 tablespoons red-wine vinegar
3 tablespoons cider vinegar
2/3 cup red grape juice
1 tablespoon chopped fresh parsley
1 teaspoon French mustard
Pinch sugar
Salt and pepper

Peel and crush garlic. Into a bowl, put garlic, oil, vinegars, grape juice, parsley, mustard, sugar, salt, and pepper.

Whisk ingredients together until thoroughly mixed. Alternatively, put all ingredients in a clean jelly jar. Screw top on jar and shake until ingredients are thoroughly mixed together.

Adjust seasoning before serving. Serve the dressing with a mixed bean salad or cooked vegetables.

Makes 1-1/2 cups/24 tablespoons.

Calories per tablespoon: 28
Fat per tablespoon: 2.6 g

——SWEET & SOUR DRESSING——

1 garlic clove
1 (1-inch) piece gingerroot
1/4 cup olive oil
5 tablespoons lemon juice
5 tablespoons red-wine vinegar
2 tablespoons honey
2 tablespoons soy sauce
2 tablespoons ketchup
2 tablespoons medium-dry sherry
1 tablespoon sesame seeds
Pinch red (cayenne) pepper
Salt and pepper

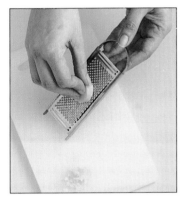

Peel and crush garlic. Peel and chop or grate ginger finely.

Into a bowl, put garlic, gingerroot, oil, lemon juice, vinegar, honey, soy sauce, ketchup, sherry, sesame seeds, red (cayenne) pepper, salt, and pepper. Whisk ingredients together until thoroughly mixed.

Alternatively, put all ingredients in a clean jelly jar. Screw top on jar and shake until ingredients are thoroughly mixed. Adjust seasoning before serving. Serve with fresh salad leaves, a seafood salad, or a chicken salad.

Makes 1-1/2 cups/24 tablespoons.

Calories per tablespoon: 35
Fat per tablespoon: 3 g

─── HERBY CHEESE DRESSING ───

1 garlic clove
1 cup low-fat cream cheese
2/3 cup sour cream
2 tablespoons chopped fresh mixed herbs, such as
    parsley, chives, rosemary, and thyme
1 tablespoon lemon juice
Salt and pepper

Peel and crush garlic. Into a bowl, put garlic, cream cheese, cream, herbs, lemon juice, salt, and pepper.

Whisk ingredients together until thoroughly mixed. Cover and leave dressing in a cool place 30 minutes before serving to let flavors develop.

Adjust seasoning before serving. Serve with fresh salad leaves, raw or cooked vegetables, a pasta salad, or a beef salad.

Makes 1-1/2 cups/24 tablespoons.

Calories per tablespoon: 31
Fat per tablespoon: 2.7 g

— TOMATO-YOGURT DRESSING —

1 shallot
8 ounces tomatoes
1 tablespoon low-fat margarine
1-1/4 cups low-fat plain yogurt
2 tablespoons chopped fresh basil
Salt and pepper

Using a sharp knife, chop shallot finely. Peel and chop tomatoes finely. In a saucepan over low heat, melt margarine.

Add shallot and tomatoes and cook 5 to 10 minutes or until soft, stirring. Remove pan from heat and set aside to cool.

In a bowl, stir together cooled tomato mixture, yogurt, basil, salt, and pepper until thoroughly mixed. Adjust seasoning before serving. Serve with fresh salad leaves, pasta or egg salad, or smoked fish, such as smoked mackerel.

Makes 2 cups/32 tablespoons.

Calories per tablespoon: 8
Fat per tablespoon: 0.3 g

—MINT & YOGURT DRESSING—

1 garlic clove
1-1/4 cups low-fat plain yogurt
2 tablespoons low-fat milk
2 tablespoons chopped fresh mint
Salt and pepper

Peel and crush garlic. Into a bowl, put garlic, yogurt, milk, mint, salt, and pepper.

Whisk ingredients together until thoroughly mixed. Cover and leave dressing in a cool place 30 minutes before serving to let flavors develop. Adjust seasoning before serving.

Serve with a mixed bean salad or chicken salad.

Makes 1-1/2 cups/24 tablespoons.

Calories per tablespoon: 8
Fat per tablespoon: 0.1 g

Variation: In place of garlic and mint, add finely grated zest and juice of 1 lemon or 1 lime.

ORANGE-CINNAMON DRESSING

2/3 cup unsweetened orange juice
6 tablespoons white-wine vinegar
1/4 cup sunflower oil
Finely grated zest and juice of 1 orange
1 teaspoon ground cinnamon
Salt and pepper

Into a bowl, put orange juice, vinegar, oil, orange zest and squeezed juice, cinnamon, salt, and pepper. Beat ingredients together until thoroughly mixed.

Alternatively, place all ingredients in a clean jelly jar. Screw top on jar and shake until all ingredients are thoroughly mixed together.

Adjust seasoning before serving. Serve with fresh salad leaves, pasta salad, cooked or raw vegetables, or cold, sliced pork.

Makes 1-1/4 cups/20 tablespoons.

Calories per tablespoon: 30
Fat per tablespoon: 3 g

Variation: Use all freshly squeezed orange juice extra flavor.

— APPLE-YOGURT DRESSING —

1 pound eating apples
1-1/4 cups low-fat plain yogurt
1 ounce preserved ginger
2 tablespoons syrup from ginger
2 tablespoons sweet sherry or apple liqueur
White pepper, to taste

Peel, core, and slice apples thinly. Into a saucepan, put apples with 3 tablespoons water. Cover and cook until apples are soft, stirring occasionally.

Remove pan from heat and mash apples thoroughly with a fork or potato masher. Set aside to cool. In a bowl, whisk together cooled applesauce and yogurt.

Chop ginger finely and whisk into yogurt mixture along with ginger syrup, sherry or apple liqueur, and white pepper to taste. Mix ingredients together well and adjust seasoning before serving. Serve with a crisp fresh salad or sliced cooked meats, such as ham or pork.

Makes 2-3/4 cups/44 tablespoons.

Calories per tablespoon: 10
Fat per tablespoon: 0.07 g

—GARLIC & GINGER DRESSING—

2 garlic cloves
1 (1-inch) piece fresh gingerroot
7 tablespoons cider vinegar
2 tablespoons light soy sauce
1 tablespoon sunflower oil
1 tablespoon sesame oil
Salt and pepper

Peel and crush garlic cloves. Peel and chop or grate ginger finely.

Into a bowl, put garlic, ginger, vinegar, soy sauce, sunflower oil, sesame oil, salt, and pepper. Beat ingredients together until thoroughly mixed. Alternatively, put all ingredients in a clean jelly jar. Screw top on jar and shake until all the ingredients are thoroughly mixed.

Adjust seasoning before serving. Serve with a fresh mixed salad, root vegetables, a mixed bean salad, or broiled chicken or turkey.

Makes 3/4 cup/12 tablespoons.

Calories per tablespoon: 28
Fat per tablespoon: 2.7 g

— CILANTRO & LIME DRESSING —

2/3 cup white grape juice
6 tablespoons white-wine vinegar
1/4 cup sunflower oil
2 tablespoons chopped fresh cilantro
Finely grated zest of 1 lime
Juice of 2 limes
1 teaspoon sugar
Salt and pepper

Into a bowl, put grape juice, vinegar, oil, cilantro, lime rind, lime juice, sugar, salt, and pepper.

Beat ingredients together until thoroughly mixed. Alternatively, put all ingredients in a clean jelly jar. Screw top on jar and shake until all ingredients are thoroughly mixed together.

Adjust seasoning before serving. Serve with fresh salad leaves, fish, or cold, sliced cooked meats.

Makes 1-1/2 cups/24 tablespoons.

Calories per tablespoon: 28
Fat per tablespoon: 2.6 g

Variation: In place of the lime zest and juice, use lemon or orange zest and a mixture of chopped fresh herbs, such as parsley, thyme, and basil.

— BANANA-YOGURT DRESSING —

2 bananas
1-1/4 cups low-fat plain yogurt
3 tablespoons honey
1/4 teaspoon apple pie spice

Peel and slice bananas and put them in a bowl. Mash bananas thoroughly with a fork or potato masher.

Add yogurt, honey, and apple pie spice to bowl and stir ingredients together until well mixed. Cover and leave sauce in a cool place 30 minutes before serving to let flavors develop.

Serve with fresh salad leaves, a pasta salad, or a mixed fruit and vegetable salad.

Makes 2-1/4 cups/36 tablespoons.

Calories per tablespoon: 14
Fat per tablespoon: 0.09 g

Variation: In place of apple pie spice, add 1/4 teaspoon ground ginger to dressing.

——RASPBERRY VINAIGRETTE——

1 (14-oz.) can raspberries packed in light syrup
1/2 cup red-wine vinegar
5 tablespoons sunflower oil
1 teaspoon sugar
1 teaspoon dried sage
Salt and pepper

Into a blender or food processor, put raspberries and juice and blend until smooth.

Strain raspberry puree through a nylon
strainer and discard seeds. Into a bowl, put
raspberry juice, vinegar, oil, sugar, sage, salt,
and pepper. Beat ingredients together until
thoroughly mixed.

Alternatively, put all ingredients in a clean
jelly jar. Screw top on jar and shake until
ingredients are thoroughly mixed. Adjust
seasoning before serving. Serve with fresh
salad leaves, a rice salad, avocado, or cold,
sliced cooked meats such as chicken.

Makes 2-1/4 cups/36 tablespoons.

Calories per tablespoon: 30
Fat per tablespoon: 2.3 g

—FRESH TARRAGON DRESSING—

3/4 cup low-fat cream cheese
2/3 cup reduced-fat light cream or low-fat yogurt
2 tablespoons chopped fresh tarragon
1 tablespoon tarragon vinegar
Salt and pepper

Into a bowl, put cream cheese and cream or yogurt and mix together well.

Stir in tarragon, vinegar, salt, and pepper, mixing together well. Cover and leave dressing in a cool place 30 minutes before serving to let flavors develop. Adjust seasoning before serving.

Serve with asparagus or hot or cold sliced cooked meats, such as chicken or turkey.

Makes 1-1/3 cups/21 tablespoons.

Calories per tablespoon: 24
Fat per tablespoon: 1.9 g

Variation: Use low-fat milk in place of the cream or yogurt, for an even lower-calorie/ lower-fat dressing.

Calories per tablespoon: 18
Fat per tablespoon: 1.3 g

INDEX